FRANK W. CAVANAUGH

INSIDE FOOTBALL

Ether Editors

ETHER EDITIONS

Inside Football by Major Frank W. Cavanaugh (1876-1933) was originally published in Boston, Massachusetts by Small, Maynard and Company Publishers in 1919.

The period illustrations appearing in this edition are from the Prints and Photographs Division of the Library of Congress in Washington, D.C.

The biographical sketch entitled "Major Frank W. Cavanaugh" appearing at the end of this edition is Copyright 2023 by Ether Editions.

CONTENTS

CONTENTS

CONTENTS

CONTENTS

ILLUSTRATIONS

INSIDE FOOTBALL

*To the memory of the many football men of America
who gave their lives in their country's service
during the war against the imperial governments
of Germany and Austria-Hungary,
this book is dedicated.*

PREFACE

All my other Octobers, I thought, had been so unlike and yet so like to this one. The smell of saddle leather was vaguely evocative of that odor of new footballs which sets the memories of many seasons flowing. In the air was the same crisp tang of other autumns, and beneath our feet the rustle of withered leaves. From beyond the hill we could hear the clanking and grinding of artillery. Before us the long hillside fell away to a shining river. Beyond, the far horizon was lit with lightning flashes, not out of heaven but out of an inferno of man's making. And from above rained down the light and radiance of other worlds. It seemed very strange to be so far away from home and fireside, very singular to find oneself present amid surroundings so weird, so unreal. It seemed very strange indeed to be directing a squad of cannoneers instead of a squad of football players. Strangest of all, came the certainty that it was very much the same thing after all, that the little problems and perplexities were very like indeed to the old problems and perplexities. "Football," I reflected, "is very like warfare, after all, and warfare would be very like football, were there as much intelligence in it. There is more intelligence," I added, "in one football game, badly though it may be played, however disgusting to the coaches, than there is in a whole war;" for it seemed to me that of intelligence in modern warfare there was very little, that the music of Mars is a mad music, that his votaries are filled with a certain witlessness, and go blind and blundering into battle like men who know not what they do. Then my thought strayed and roamed among the men around me, the men in olive drab, who had won the headgear and jersey of the other Octobers. I could always pick them out, the football players, although many there were who, never having played the grand old game, nevertheless had plenty of muscular control, good discipline, coolness under fire and cheerfulness in adversity. "These men," I reflected, "would have made good football players; it is only that they never had sufficient opportunity to play it." I thought of the heavy percentage of rejections from our army and navy recruiting stations, and that very few of the men thus humiliated had been football players. The ex-players, to be sure, were picked men originally; but there seemed to me to be no valid excuse for such a large proportion of downright inferiority. "Athletics, and especially football, would have spared many of our young men this shame," was my mental conclusion, and I added: "After this war we shall hear a cry for universal drill and military preparation; but universal athletics, and especially football, would hit nearer the mark. There is nothing like our football that I know of to make a young man alert and receptive, active and courageous; and possession of these qualities is worth, for preparedness' sake, a year's output of the Bethlehem munitions works or a lifetime spent in drilling. After the war," I said, "we shall play a lot of football, and it will not be played in a mollycoddle spirit. We shall have better football, if we can find a sufficient number of coaches who know the game. Many coaches will be needed, and, moreover, we ought to make an immediate effort to restandardize our football; for there is too much confusion among us, too much bewilderment. A consistent theory of the whole art of football, if stated, would have at least the merit of being consistent. If sound, it should aid in the standardization of our football, and if unsound, at least it might provoke a sound and thorough criticism, which leads to the same thing. A book written with this in mind should prove invaluable," I decided, "but I do not imagine that I shall have the opportunity to write it. I shall keep the thought in mind, however."

CHAPTER I: BEGINNING THE SEASON

A new coach's first talk to a squad is the one which makes the deepest impression on the largest number. This coach will never have a better opportunity to set his pupils thinking on a high plane. They should be reminded that the season beginning at the college or school calls for sacrifice, endurance, the exercise of willpower and pride in bodily and mental improvement, including the maintenance of a high standard of scholarship. The season must be one of cooperation, unity of purpose, concentration, teamwork and unselfishness in the commonly accepted meaning of that term. Urge all members of the squad, moreover, to discourage chronic wet-blankets and objectors who have no remedies to offer, whether members of the squad or outsiders. Players with new ideas, moreover, should be encouraged to impart them to the coach. I have sometimes told a squad at the first meeting: "If you are not willing to sacrifice an arm or a leg for the good of the cause — not that anyone hopes or expects or desires that such a sacrifice be made — the cause is not sufficiently serious to you, and you ought not to be on the squad."

It is not to be intimated, or understood, that any coach would be so self-seeking, or any school expect so much, that any man should be called upon to sacrifice the equivalent of a limb. It is not to be presumed that a coach would be so brutal as to take any unnecessary chances with his men. But it is entirely reasonable to require that men of the caliber desired for a football team be willing to make such a sacrifice.

A team should have the do-or-die spirit. If a game of this nature is not important enough to fight for, it would be a travesty on sport to play it at all. Here, then, is the beautiful school in which sacrifice for an ideal is taught, developed and made a part of the man. Strange as it may seem to the fanatics of rest, peace and quiet enjoyment, the large majority of the men who are thus taught come to love the lesson and its teacher.

Keep the players on the field in a serious frame of mind. Contrary to a prevalent opinion, enthusiastic football students can maintain and increase that enthusiasm by sustained application more readily than by a diversion of frivolity and relaxation. The squad should include men of a serious and studious turn of mind, who, even if they are not of varsity timber, will encourage their fellows to bring up important questions as they arise. A one-man team is seldom a winner. That two heads are better than one is a good adage, but eleven heads are even better; that is to say, eleven thinkers, not eleven leaders; for there should be only one quarterback or captain, too many frogs muddling the football puddle very decidedly.

While the serious attitude of the players should never be discouraged, there are times at mid-season when the going is hard and men easily become irritable. Under such conditions, the coach should make special opportunity for less serious play, never riotous or risky, but based on forms of light exercise such as all men know. These games may be relied upon to rekindle naturally happy dispositions, in order to build up a mental reserve for the especially severe grind at the end of the season.

Discipline is a very important habit to form early, or it will never become a fact. Before any practice is attempted the men should be informed that they must not and shall not be late to meals or practice. Delay in dressing before or after practice should not be countenanced. A football team cannot become a well drilled and disciplined machine without insistence upon the trifles, so called. The spirit of a squad that gets out early and with snap at the start of the season is always superior.

There should be a preliminary exercise of calisthenics, to loosen the muscles and warm the body (but not for body and arms alone, with the legs in a rigid position). The legs must also be encouraged to work with the mind. Leg exercises, with the legs in a crouched position, have no merit; as it has been historically demonstrated to a convincing degree that a quick man can get a slow, heavy man out of the way.

The main idea should be to keep all the men moving all the time, except when they are listening to instruction; as a busy squad acquires a much more convincing sense of duty well done, with its accompanying mental satisfactions, as well as a keener and earlier awakening to the fact that somebody is taking care of it who knows his business.

The preliminary practice should be conducted in accordance with a schedule, but that schedule should be reconstructed if it is found to be inadequate. No matter how large the squad, every man should be kept occupied, one group tackling or blocking at the dummy, another falling on the ball, others going through signals, others punting or passing. The fundamentals are the essentials. Once positively and firmly grounded, the team, with any reasonable opportunity, will grow and develop.

Everybody is an end and everybody is a pass thrower and a punter as well, for the first three or four days of preliminary conditioning; days divided, if possible, into forenoon and afternoon workouts of short duration, with vigilant watchfulness exercised against overexertion or excessive fatigue. Short tossing of the ball and fielding of the same gives every man a good stretch. These tosses should have a maximum of twenty-five yards, and there should be exchanges of punts at the same distance, with attention to form both in punting and catching. The wearing of very tight clothing is advisable during these early sessions, often undertaken during one of summer's late revivals; and all candidates should be warned to report fatigue or the slightest lameness in arm or leg.

The players may be divided into squads of a dozen, and sent ambling around the field, throwing the ball from one to another; perhaps choosing sides and making a semi-basketball affair out of it, but always with a sharp eye to exhaustion.

After the first day, pick out any of the possible heavy men who might become centers or sub-centers, and put quarterback candidates behind them. Show the latter the positions to assume with a view to forward passes, while standing in various receiving positions at various distances. Show the Centers how to make passes, including the spiral pass, which cannot, however, be relied upon exclusively, because of its impracticability on muddy days. Then start the handling of the ball, sending ends down under the resulting passes, which should be so short that they can be fielded without strain, but long enough to develop handling and fielding the ball, and also return throwing.

Gradually increase the distances, both of the forward passing and the punting. Summer punters, whose legs are already in fair shape, may begin to get length on their kicks, and the army of "ends," including tackles and guards in the making, will begin to go down under kicks and passes faster, though less frequently, walking back along the sidelines to make place for the next set of forwards which comes clattering down under the punt.

The receivers should practice a smart getaway after catching, but should play it safe, first making sure of the catch. The ball is received on the solar plexus, to bound out slightly against the left hand and drop into the right hand held underneath to complete the pocket. Punt receivers should bind the first two and also the third and fourth fingers together with tape, thus avoiding nine-tenths of the early season finger injuries incidental to punt catching. It is well to remember, incidentally, that a really sore knuckle or toe becomes almost painless if bound to its neighbor for support. Tagging the receiver takes the place of tackling in preliminary down-the-field work, but the punt-catchers should begin immediately to practice the use of the straight arm and the use of the free arm by the side to break a man's tackle.

On the fourth day of practice, start the men falling from a standing position on a stationary football contained in a small circle six feet away; paying special attention to form. After a few days this specialty can be practiced with the man running and the ball in motion. Teach the player to go over the ball straight, after the manner of a down-swooping hydroplane, running lower and lower with each stride, until the final plunge has more of a skimming than a falling motion. The player's body, with shoulders equidistant from the ground, should barely avoid grazing the ball. He completes its recovery by turning over upon either hip, as comes most natural to him, at the same time pulling in the ball so that the upper legs and lower body form a right-angled pocket, which the arms complete.

Players should not be asked to fall on the ball in twos, threes or fours until after the first game, or after a fair amount of scrimmage work. Many men seem to reserve all their natural and acquired clumsiness for this operation, which to other football players presents no more difficulty than a kitten experiences while at play with a ball of yarn. Clumsy men injure themselves and injure others; and falling on the ball, although a highly essential specialty to acquire, is watched with misgivings by coaches and trainers, who never know when an accident may occur. The risks are apparently heavier than in scrimmage itself, and yet a great majority of natural football players fall on the ball year after year without suffering the slightest injury.

Quick starts and quick stops, both so necessary in football, may be practiced at an early stage in the season. Never give so many starts that the element of speed is lost through fatigue. Rest as often as necessary; but get the genuine snap into both the starting and the stopping. Develop the utmost in muscular response to brain command.

Shadow dodging is another important means of developing rapid coordination and bringing out natural dodging speed. For this exercise twenty to thirty posts or sticks should be set up at irregular intervals within a square measuring fifteen yards on each side. Players should learn to dodge by running at speed through this maze of obstacles, avoiding the latter and also one another by complete turns of the body. Accomplished and highly elusive dodgers tend to run with restraint, and should therefore be given at least their full share of work in falling on the ball, and tackling the dummy.

Begin to use the dummy after three or four days of preliminary exercise. Men learn at the dummy how to block in interference, as well as tackling, but it is well to postpone blocking exercises until after the first two or three scrimmages. Heart and enthusiasm make the tackle, but at the dummy he can be taught to watch the knees and lower legs rather than the head. The coach meanwhile should impress his own interest, thoroughness and "pep" on the tackler, arousing as much enthusiasm as possible by his voice — in order to solace the novice for his skinned elbows. The coach should instill also the spirit of rivalry and fight by the voice, by comparisons, and by the trend of his conversation.

From the first day of practice the coach should use a large blackboard for instruction in signals, formations, and plays. Three basic plays, which can be worked on either side of the line, will, with the punt, give him a total of seven plays to serve as the foundation of his working offense. These plays should be explained in full detail to the squad. Each man should learn not only where he goes and what he does, but also the individual assignment of every man on the team. The coach must have in his own mind a very clear and precise reasoning of what each player is to do on every play, and he must know his plays as he knows his alphabet; else, under cross-examination, his prestige will suffer an enormous decline. If the slightest changes are made later in any play, the changes must be explained and learned as thoroughly as the original moves. Further plays should be added to these as fast as the squad can assimilate them. The system of signals which will govern the plays should be expounded in as clear and concise a manner as possible. The signals themselves must be the simplest possible and the most easily changed on short notice. Put the signals on the blackboard, and drive them home with diagrams of the plays. Then, on the field, line up the squad into teams on attack. Let the teams walk through the plays, at first, against a wholly imaginary defense; each man, however, taking out, blocking off or charging back the invisible opponent assigned to him.

Scales, stakes, rope, blackboard and dummy are the principal inanimate devices which new coaches will find most serviceable and necessary in teaching football.

In addition to a setting-up drill at the start of practice, a calisthenic exercise at the end of the day is advisable, especially if the men have been spending considerable time in listening to instruction. The practice should conclude with a sprint to the training house, rather than with a long run. It appears to be a general practice to scrimmage men, or work them otherwise, as far as the men can go, and then send them on long runs. This is a wholly unnecessary hardship. If men, after practice, are still capable of long runs, with no atom of interest in the performance, it seems much more advisable to prolong the instruction in practical football.

Every man on the squad should have a proper amount of work each day, and if there are substitutes who have been of necessity neglected, and if darkness has fallen so that further coaching is rendered impossible, the long run may serve a useful purpose; but players generally regard it as merely a form of torture. The proof is not far to seek. It is only necessary to take a football squad and send it for a mile on the track after an average afternoon's work. Watch the men's faces as they run and their attitude when they finish. Then the next night call the men together at the end of the practice and say: "That's all for tonight. Now, then, everybody sprint for the gym!" After the long run the men were worn out and silent. Tonight they are happy, full of life and off with a live step and a joyous heart for the showers.

Occasionally a coach may order a run as one of the surprises which are such a great element in holding attention, whether always pleasant, or now and then disagreeable. Even the disagreeable surprise will arouse interest, and the long run easily includes itself in a list of the disagreeables. Unless a man's attendance is required for study purposes, he should be sent at once to the dressing room after taking him out of a practice, especially in chilly weather. He can get from his bath, if taken immediately, a snap and a revival not to be expected if his body is allowed to chill in the bitter autumn breezes. Men on the field, once they start exercising, should be kept busy, and there is always plenty for them to do. They must get accustomed to falling on the ground and to protecting their muscles and conserving their wind and endurance as a matter of second nature, before they are ready for football. It is the trainer's business and the coach's business, meanwhile, to see to it that no man in practice exerts himself to the limit; watching especially the new men who report late, but watching, also, the varying weights of all the men, and turning all suspected cases of organic disturbance over to the physician, before it becomes too late.

CHAPTER II: THE WARRIOR'S ARMOR

In the general sense I am not in favor of heavy, burdensome protective devices. Whatever protection is used should be particularly chosen with a view to strength and lightness. A man can be injured by first becoming exhausted through carrying too many pounds of pads and braces, for even these are insufficient if the wearer's muscles are relaxed from excessive fatigue. In addition to the protection which every athlete provides for himself, no football man should ever go on the field for a scrimmage or a game without a headgear. It neither makes a coward out of him to wear one nor a braver man to go without. If for no other reason, over a span of ten years the headgear will take away from the alarmists many opportunities to cry down football. Many cuts requiring stitches, and other serious head injuries, are avoided by wearing headgear. There is no penalty of discomfort from wearing this protection and no psychological disadvantage.

Shoulder braces of light, substantial material should be used for the protection of the scapula. Light hip pads for the top of the hip bone afford some protection also to the floating ribs. These pads are sewn inside the trousers, and protrude above in semicircular shape. Light kidney pads of leather faced felt are similarly adjusted. Thigh pads are fitted into pockets on the front and inside of the trouser legs. The kneecap should be protected by a light pad contained in the roll of the trouser leg and a thin, flat sponge is preferable to a pad. The sponge should be wet, most of the water then being squeezed out. It is very light, but offers remarkable protective resistance.

As a rule, shin guards do not appear to be necessary. They have nearly gone out of use. Yet I would recommend them strongly for occasional men who have supersensitive shins. If a man is more comfortable with shin guards, let him wear them; and the same applies to nose guards. I would specially urge very low-cut shoes for all players. Were it not for the ankle bone, I would have them cut as low as the summer Oxford. Since 1898 until comparatively recent years, when I found an athletic goods house which would make them at short notice as I wanted them, I used to cut down the standard football shoes before they were served out so that the upper would extend no higher than the middle of the ankle bone.

These shoes were intended to protect the ankle, and often reached the calf of the leg. When such a shoe was laced tightly it gave a decided sensation of protection, an impression which the player carried into the game with him. As the ankle worked about in the shoe, the pressure of the laces readjusted itself, the result being increased tightness around the top of the shoe. The wearer still used his ankle as if it were braced, though it now had no brace whatever. The result was an extraordinary number of sprained ankles. Cutting the shoe down and lacing it tightly over the instep, giving no brace whatever to the ankle, forced this joint to do its work and protect itself. I cannot recall three cases of sprained ankle in fifteen years of coaching.

Of course, the man who steps into a hidden hole on a football field is liable to a sprain, but nothing will ever be invented to prevent an accident of this kind, if the freedom of the joint is to be considered.

The group photographs in the football guide show not one team in twenty uniformed with canvas jackets; variously padded and camouflaged jerseys being apparently very much in the mode. This fashion appears to me to involve a somewhat thought-less sacrifice of efficiency. Canvas jackets should by all means be worn, as the jersey is a hundred per cent easier to grasp. If it is a good jersey it will stretch without tearing. An unbroken hold on a jersey by a man of reasonable strength will catch the wearer with one leg in the air and snap him back as if the jersey were a powerful spring.

Within recent years I have seen two touchdowns lost in impor-tant games in this manner. In one case the ball was carried to a point directly over the goal line, if not slightly beyond it, when the runner was snapped back without ceremony. In the excitement, the referee either failed to notice that the ball had been actually carried to a point where, under the rules, a touchdown should have been awarded, or else lost his nerve. Anyway the next lineup took place six feet from the goal line. One finds it difficult to censure the official too severely, considering how difficult it was to believe one's own eyes as to the elasticity of a jersey and the distance the runner's sudden recoil had covered.

The jacket should be tightly laced, with due regard to freedom of breathing. Good results can be obtained by fitting the men to jackets and trousers separately, and then having the garments united by a tailor so that the whole will fit the body perfectly, and give entire freedom of action. Elastic material is generally used to effect the union. If the team's treasury can afford it, have a special shoe for muddy fields, rigged with three long cleats under the ball of the foot, as far apart as possible, so as to give them the least chance to hold caked earth. Place at most two cleats of the same kind on the heel. Drop-kickers cannot use these mud cleats, and this is a small point to remember.

I have found it particularly worth while to equip backs and ends with a special light shoe for their important games. These shoes by their very nature are not guaranteed to stand a season's work, but imagination when well directed is a fine thing to cater to, and the extra life and dash exhibited by players thus equipped is positive. Stockings should have white feet — regardless of the college color; this as a safeguard against infection. Even better, players might wear short white socks under the stockings. Blankets of good quality and generous size should be a part of the team's equipment. They should be used during all long waits, even when the weather is not cold. Chewing gum (or equivalents) should be discouraged during practice or a game. Chewing increases rather than diminishes thirst. Do not forget to give the players a swallow of water between periods. Between the halves hot coffee, with or without milk and sugar, is a better stimulant than drug or dram. Bar positively the powerful drugs. A man's future is more important than even football.

CHAPTER III: THE TACKLING DUMMY

I have watched carefully the charging machine, the bucking strap, and many other mechanical devices, employed to develop football players. In the first place, they are abhorrent to me. They suggest the training of a dog for a dog fight. They cannot by any chance elevate the moral standards of the man. Generally speaking, I have a great aversion for this manner of development. After two decades of observation and experimentation, I am convinced that it is inferior and inadvisable. Work of this sort is drudgery, and tends to deaden the imagination. It is unreal, and just different enough from the actual combat against live forces to raise a question as to its efficacy, even disregarding its other undesirable features.

The charging machine, although novel and astonishing, I have never even considered. There are those who claim that practice upon the charging machine develops rhythm and unity of charge. Undoubtedly this is true, to a questionable degree. But the machine has no individuality, no comeback, stands dead waiting for the attack; and the men charging it, not being interested and soon becoming fatigued, learn instinctively to keep the rhythm and the unity of charge while slowly but surely discarding the most important things, snap and speed. Unless it is absolutely necessary, it is poor judgment to order young, intelligent men to attack an inanimate object, where there is a complete lack of the thrill of personal contact or the danger of prompt and effective retaliation. Signal drills develop unity of charge sufficiently, and this without building slow, heavy muscles.

The man running into a bucking strap springs like an animal; leaps into it, tearing up the ground, and struggles and fights like a trapped beast. If the man has any individuality or the fire of freedom in his soul, he is mentally registering a protest against his degradation. The prayer for these devices is that they develop muscle. But in the various phases of football there is no end to the interesting work that can be given to a football man which will develop muscle as fast as he can put it on, at the same time developing enthusiasm. The only chance one has to retain the respect of the man who is in the bucking strap, and to preserve for him his own, is by the weak and ineffectual use of compliment or flattery; weak especially in this case because the man's physical position, bound up as he is, is too base to enable him to respond to either. There is no element of personal combat. Those who are holding the ends of the strap have an overwhelming advantage if they care to exercise it; and they are not in any sense considered as antagonists by the halfback who straggles in the throes of a ridiculous endeavor. They are often two of the most useless members of the squad: a clincher against arousing any enthusiasm on the bucker's part.

Now the tackling dummy is a necessary evil. It is open to many of the same objections registered against the charging machine and the bucking strap. But a most compelling argument for the dummy is that because of the need for constant practice in tackling and blocking, the exclusive use of members of the squad in lieu of the stuffed image would develop more injuries than the squad could afford. It is a strange phenomenon that when the dummy is discarded in favor of tackling practice against real men carrying the ball so many should be injured, both runners and tacklers, whereas in games or scrimmage practice injuries from this cause are infrequent.

Undoubtedly this difference is attributable to the added zest of real play as against feature practice. Increased enthusiasm makes for a disregard of possible injury, which, in turn, means a full, natural muscular pressure, the best possible insurance against injury. Lack of interest means an attitude mentally conservative, which results in muscular conservatism. This is a natural shrinking of the muscles from their full duty, thereby exposing ligaments, tissues, bones and tendons to shock.

"Tackling Dummy"
Bain News Service

Tackling the dummy by no means teaches the complete lesson of tackling. It trains the man, however, to throw himself at the object from either foot, until the movement becomes instinctive and any natural or possible hesitation is removed. The same may be said of blocking on the dummy. Accurate tackling and blocking are more or less instinctive in an enthusiastic player. What the dummy does is to give the first lessons in form. It teaches that both tackling and blocking are reasonably easy. It relieves the beginner of fear or misapprehension with regard to safety from injury when the dummy is missed, or when, for any reason, the player falls into clumsy or uncontrollable positions.

Successful tackling gives perhaps the most wonderful and satisfying sensation that football provides. Success is based on the lesson, well learned, to watch the runner's knees; second, good muscular control on the part of the tackier; third, enthusiasm; and fourth, the determination to go through the man, not to the man; in other words to assume that the runner must be reached a foot to two feet beyond where he is actually seen to be.

To be sure, there are other necessary qualifications but they appear to be included in those already given. Muscular control involves the instinctive turning of the head away from the runner's knee. There is a law, both written and unwritten, that a tackier should throw his body across, and in front of the runner. For years I have seen this method taught, practiced and accomplished; but I question if I have ever seen a man who tackled in this fashion who was able for long to keep out of the infirmary or the hospital. The idea is as pernicious as it is foolish.

Of course, there are times when a man finds himself in such a position, and compelled to act so quickly, that he has no choice in the matter. The head is the directing force, physically as well as mentally, after the final lunge has been made. It should be pointed directly at the objective point of the final lunge. If at the runner's knees, the tackier must learn to turn his head while tackling, so as to avoid unnecessary punishment. Such punishment cannot be avoided if the player persists in throwing his head across the pathway of the runner.

CHAPTER IV: SCRIMMAGE AND CORRECTIONS

Scrimmage practice should begin as early as possible, and naturally a team will require and desire two or three such sessions before entering its first game. The early scrimmages are so often interrupted for purposes of explanation that plenty of respite is provided; but the coach and trainer should keep a sharp eye on the physical condition of the players. Many an exhausted player has suffered because a coach has said to himself: "We'll try a few more plays; the men are tired, but they need the work." The blackboard and explanations on the field should be used in place of scrimmage so far as possible.

The bulk of the scrimmage work necessary should be completed early in the season, to discover material, develop the men's ideas and arouse the spirit of competition; also to harden the players and for the sake of the teaching of football possible only in scrimmage. Minor or more serious injuries sustained in scrimmage will have all the more time to mend before the important games if the bulk of the scrimmage work is done early. Having acquired the idea and habit of scrimmage, it will be better for the players later in the season to go into their games with a little less knowledge but also without the sore spots, than with a little more knowledge plus the sore spots. The latter lead unconsciously to a defensive attitude which may result in fresh and unnecessary injuries.

Coaches in charge of scrimmage practice should specialize upon thoroughness to the last detail. Monday should be a corrective day if there has been a Saturday game; a limbering-up day for the men who played half the game or more, and a scrimmage day for the remaining substitutes, if there are enough of them and also enough competent coaching available to superintend their work. Tuesday and Thursday are generally the best scrimmage days for the first-string men. The line men should also be scrimmaged on Wednesday, holding out the ends and backs. This statement presupposes a larger number of substitutes than many school teams possess. But a coach should not overdo scrimmage whether his squad is large or small. There is plenty of very necessary detail work that can be put on when it seems inadvisable to scrimmage.

Every team has a game during the first half of the season when the tackling is ragged. When the players reassemble on the following Monday, I usually indulge in a few remarks concerning individual and collective shortcomings, explaining that they attempted to reach runners with their arms, instead of driving with their shoulders to "the man beyond the man;" or that they watched the runner's upper body, instead of his knees and feet, before making the final swoop. I then designate a certain day in the near future as "Bloody Wednesday," or "Bloody Thursday," as the case may be, notifying the squad of the nature of the intended celebration.

A portion of the afternoon in question is used to send unfortunate substitutes down the line with footballs, also with full liberty and license to go at any speed possible, and to use as much of the field as they may require. The varsity players should make four or five tackles apiece without shirking the test in any respect. The wild man in the open usually proves sufficiently elusive and determined to make the test entirely valid.

It is a tough game, and hard on the team. There may be a few bruises and sore spots at nightfall. But it generally serves, a few suitable invectives aiding, to put the team on its mettle; at least to put it in a spirit of determination to avoid occasion for other bloody days. "Bloody Thursday" is not without its psychological value, and it certainly provides one of the hardest tests of tackling, which is more a matter of spirit than of skill.

I have been asked a hundred times what I do to eradicate fumbling. I always answer: "Nothing." Develop good passes and a fighting team and the fumbling will take care of itself. A team may, and probably will, suffer from fumbling in a violently epidemic form, at some stage of its career, but it will recover. Fortunately, the one bad day usually occurs early in the season. To harp on the subject excessively might create a permanent nervous habit. A coach may take it for granted that his players do not desire to fumble, and that they will cure themselves of the tendency, time aiding, if he keeps cool himself.

"Line Up for a Punt-Out!"
Harris & Ewing

This is not at all the same thing as saying that a coach can never give an individual a helpful suggestion which will enable him to make his own corrections. For instance, if you have a punt-catcher who muffs, although his general form seems to be good, look and see if he does not catch with too wide a straddle. If so, his basket has no bottom to it. On the same principle, teach punt-catchers not to draw away from the ball as they would from a fast liner in baseball, where a player is taught to yield with the catch.

Quizzes on the rules should be held frequently early in the season, and not omitted late in the season. Insist, particularly, that the men learn the penalties. This is a very good way to teach the game, as a matter of fact, for there is a great deal of football wrapped up in the definitions of offenses, and players show at least a certain degree of curiosity to find out what may happen to them in case they do commit any forbidden action. Every member of the squad should be provided with a rule book. It is unfortunately true that most of these choicely illustrated volumes will be thrown away, possibly in consequence of the inborn horror of books which brought their possessors to college or school. But a few men, at least, on every squad will prove apt students and able football lawyers. The coach should encourage all forms of liberal education. And please teach your team how to line up for a punt-out!

CHAPTER V: THE GRASS DRILL

The grass drill I greatly prefer to the regular line of calisthenics. This drill a generation of football players at Dartmouth recall with mingled emotions, but with no lack of appreciation of the benefits they derived from it, or of the many humorous occurrences which lightened their toils when newcomers were introduced to the exercise for the first time.

The idea of the grass drill suggested itself to me in the course of a conversation with Stephen Chase, the former intercollegiate champion high hurdler and world's record holder. His spiked shoes long since laid aside, Mr. Chase was describing to me, during a train ride which found us fellow passengers, a game which he had taught to his two little boys, one three and the other five years of age.

He caused them to lie on the floor, in unnaturally tangled-up postures arranged by himself, until, at a given signal, they were to untangle themselves and jump to an erect, standing position, as speedily as possible. The prize to the winner was one cent. The most interesting part of the story to me was his statement that although at first the older boy invariably won the prize, their father was much surprised and pleased to find, at the end of two weeks, that the competition was becoming intense, the problem of deciding the winner increasingly difficult, and that the prizes were being divided on substantially a fifty-fifty basis.

After the recital of this story my first thought was that if such an increase could be brought about in the mental alertness and bodily nimbleness of a three-year-old boy by the development of his speed and the eradication of the clumsiness natural to his age, what wonders might not be performed with the big, heavy men of imperfect coordination whom coaches are perpetually and often hopelessly attempting to develop into football players. The grass drill was the result of this reflection, and I have never ceased to be thankful to the children of Stephen Chase and to their father. The pleasure which he took in their development I have been able to appreciate and share the more completely when my two hundred-pounders in green began to be able to keep up with the small, fast men of a Dartmouth squad in the exacting movements of the grass drill.

The grass drill is an extraordinary means of development for the long, heavy men, whose back muscles especially seem to need strengthening. And for all who participate in it this exercise leads to perfect muscular coordination through movements arduous but interesting, because involving both mental and physical effort besides an intense spirit of competition. The drill demands and teaches immediate response to the word of command. It has the priceless value that the test of endurance which it provides takes place under the direct supervision of the coach. The lazy man only too easily and naturally foregoes a very large percentage of the value to be derived from ordinary calisthenics; it being next to impossible for the leader to discover the lack of individual effort as the exercise is conducted. Furthermore, in calisthenics there is apt to be too much exercise while the legs are held in a rigid position. This position of the legs is especially to be avoided in football. Every effort, on the contrary, should be made to loosen the muscles of the upper leg and to increase their flexibility and snap.

To introduce the grass drill, line up the entire squad in rows six feet apart, with the men six feet apart in the rows. The commands are: Attention. Front. Right. Left. Back. Go. Faster. Slower.

Halt. Rest. "Attention" is the well-known position of a soldier, and all positions assumed on these commands except "attention" and "go" are taken with the body stretched on the ground. At the commands "front," "right," "left" and "back," the body is stretched rigidly along the ground; on the first three with the head toward the line on which the coach or drill leader is stationed. The position "back" is taken with feet to the front and head to the rear, but still at right angles to the line on which the men stood at attention.

The arms in all positions other than "attention" are purposely placed in the most clumsy and least helpful position, in order that the transitions from "back" or "front" to "left" or "right" may be rendered as difficult as possible and the muscles less frequently used brought into action. At these commands the men revolve their bodies in the fastest possible manner, never rising to the feet except at the command of "attention."

All movements are to be made with the least possible motion, exertion or wasted effort, but with the greatest possible speed. At the command "front," given while the player is standing at attention, he throws his feet behind him and falls on his stomach, at the same time folding his arms so that his hands will protrude from beneath his armpits.

If the next command is "back," the movement, when completed, finds him with the feet and head in reversed positions, the body lying supine and the arms folded behind and beneath, so that the fingertips protrude at the waist. At "right" or "left" the man rolls, revolves or drops himself, depending upon his former position, until he is lying on either his right or his left side. He throws both arms behind him, grasping one wrist with the opposite hand.

The balancing of the rigid body on either side in the position outlined is by no means easy. It calls for considerable practice and for muscular control.

Hands, body, feet, neck, everything, in fact, should be used in making the revolving and twisting movements. The purpose is to throw the body into each succeeding position with the greatest possible speed and to make it difficult to get the hands into a position to help. At the command "go," the men jump or scramble to their feet, face the line on which the drill leader stands, and begin the half dancing, half running motions of a sprinter's loosening-up exercise. This running, or rather trotting, while neither advancing nor retreating, is accompanied by high knee action. The further command "faster" increases the speed. This auxiliary command can be reiterated until the men reach their limit in rapidity of motion.

After attaining this limit it is advisable at first, by periodic commands of "slower," to decrease the speed of motion until the command "attention" is suddenly given. The command "attention," for brevity and snap, may be abbreviated to "'tention."

One of the most thrilling and wonderful exhibitions by the squad is accomplished when the men, having been given the command "go," and brought by successive stages to the highest possible development of speed, suddenly hear the command "front." After three weeks to a month of practice, the suddenness of the change from the extreme of upright activity to a prostrate position on the ground, and the ease with which it is accomplished, are amazing. One might conclude from this description that the drill is too rough, and might easily lead to broken bones. As a matter of fact, the men readily acquire the skill needed to make a perfect fall, and in six years I have never seen an injury resulting from the grass drill.

The command "rest" may be given while the men are in any position; preferably after the command "back" has been executed, or the command "attention." If the ground is dry, the former position is preferable for rest, as the relief is more complete in that position. The command "rest" should mean complete relaxation, the men merely retaining their positions on the ground or standing, according to their positions when the command is given.

Participation in this drill for one month will produce notable results, especially in the clumsy men and in the tall, heavy men. In four to six weeks the muscular development in heavy men of the long, rangy type has been amazing. The drill is very easy to learn, and can be mastered in two days when the commands are given slowly. It should be borne in mind that the exercise is severe, though in no sense dangerous, even when the command "back" is given while the men are standing at attention; therefore the men should be allowed frequent rests, and preferably when they are on the ground.

"Grass Drill"
Harris & Ewing

The mental benefits are often as pronounced as the physical. Just as a man in a football scrimmage finds himself unable to think quickly while his body occupies an unnatural position, just so participants in the grass drill find it difficult at first to follow and instantly execute the commands. Even after the drill has been thoroughly mastered, the mental processes demanded are by no means simple, as greatly increased speed is called for. Logically, the drill develops greater speed and accuracy of thought in the man, and the ability to think speedily and accurately whatever the physical dilemma.

The grass drill had been in use for six years at Dartmouth, and by Dartmouth coached teams, when America entered the world war. Army officers who had seen the exercise in operation were full of appreciation of its value as a means of conditioning soldiers, physically and mentally. The adoption of this drill for the entire forces in France was contemplated, but the almost continual rain and mud encountered abroad rendered the idea impractical as the soldier has only one suit of clothes.

Coaches who adopt the grass drill should make use of it every day, except in excessively rainy or muddy weather, in order to get the full benefit. The exercise, of course, should not be overdone. The coach stands in front, to watch the effect of the work on the men, and to see to it that each move is completed by every man. The drill can be made very interesting, and an extraordinary amount of effective exercise can be teased out of men where less salutary means would often prove mere drudgery.

CHAPTER VI: TRAINING, DIET, INJURIES, AND WATER

Careful weighing of each player on accurate scales before and after every practice will provide coach and trainer with the surest index to physical and mental condition in the squad. Care of the scales and the task of weighing should be included among the duties of painstaking assistant managers.

The players' names may be tabulated alphabetically on a large pasteboard sheet, arranged with parallel columns for each practice session, one sheet covering several weeks. Each column should be wide enough to include two sets of figures: the weight of each man going out, and his weight returning from the field. This sheet, when not in use, should be posted in plain sight in the training quarters. Its presence there helps to arouse that interest which induces men to give some serious thought to their own physical condition, with regard to proper eating, adequate sleep and systematic care of the body.

It may be argued that attention to weights may tend to breed worry in certain men and render them neurasthenic. The answer is that all red-blooded boys are so eager to make the team that each and every one of them may in any event develop neurasthenia, unless an outwardly careless treatment of all deficiencies is adopted by trainer and coach. Neurotic symptoms can be detected at the scales more promptly than anywhere else, and it is there, too, that the formula of outward carelessness can be applied most effectively. But outward carelessness should be merely the mask for proper solicitude and prompt corrective action; operative in the case of the neurotic by association with happy natures, and by tactful investigation with a view to the application of remedies which will reach the cause.

Either the coach or the trainer or at least some person in authority in the football department should be a man who will belittle all injuries to the men who receive them; who is always optimistic, while never explanatory; who will talk fight, and enlarge upon the merits of great fighters. But while talking with set purpose in a fixed direction, the trainer, in reality, will work in quite another; and a too rapid loss of weight, when not regained for the most part during the intervals of rest and sleep, is one of the danger signs which put a competent physical director instantly on watch. At least three-fourths of the weight stripped off during a day's practice should be regained overnight, excepting in the case of the excessively fleshy candidate whose poundage is being reduced by a special regime of exercise, heat and diet.

If a football man is losing too much weight on exercise and not getting enough of it back, something is wrong. Probably the man is reducing not his superfluous flesh but the useful tissues of his body, and also his stamina and nervous energy. Working like a steam engine, he has already exhausted the steam engine's supply of water, contained in his body in the fat. This fat is not entirely useless. It should be gradually converted into hard, substantial tissue, rather than stripped away.

All weights should be kept as nearly as possible at the starting point as is consistent with speed and endurance, and the man who happens to carry a thin layer of external fat at the beginning of a season should lose very little of it during the first fortnight. Thereafter his weight should tend to increase. The normal man should suffer no loss of weight after the middle of the season, except temporarily in hard scrimmages or games.

Many teams and players are still trained on the old, obsolete and highly dangerous theory that it is fatal to take liquids into the system during hard exercise. As a matter of fact, the active human body should, on the contrary, be treated like a steam engine. It should be supplied with its water for fuel purposes. If there is neither water nor fat in the system to supply energy, valuable flesh and muscle must suffer. Oatmeal water in the proportion of one to four should be supplied during practice, if men are expected to work and not to lose weight unnecessarily. During a hard practice the average man can absorb a pint of this refreshment if given to him at three or four intervals. In fact, the trainer should see to it that the men do dip their noses in the bucket, and this is especially true and especially important at mid-season. Thousands of players have become overtrained, without the knowledge of their overseers, and have been accused of falling off in their play, or even of quitting, when actually their sum total of failure could have been avoided easily by the proper use of water during practice.

Too much water, like too much of anything, is harmful. To say that a man should drink a lot of water dining or after hard practice, or a game, would be foolish. Such teaching might have dangerous consequences; but if the water is not in the system, the tissues must suffer. Therefore it is advisable, in all except specific cases of excessive weight, to lead the squad to water like animals, or as one would keep a locomotive supplied. The amount taken at one time should be small, but water should be served to the men at least thrice during the afternoon workout. A total of a pint of water, taken at intervals during practice or a game, cannot harm and must do good, while a quart and a pint additional of water taken during the remainder of the day, equaling six ordinary glasses, is not too much for a man in training.

The old theory of abstinence from water by athletes has left many failures and some wrecks along the way, and the ancient command: "Gargle, don't swallow it!" is still audible on football fields and elsewhere. It is absurd and almost criminal to see the great boxer train for his contest under extreme mental and physical pressure, rinsing his throat, religiously, instead of taking down the small swallow of water which would improve his mental and physical condition at least ten per cent. The gargle is one of the old, iron-clad customs of the dark ages. It is a horrible fallacy.

Concerning the ethical questions involved in the establishment and maintenance of a training table there has been much debate. Practically, the training table is very necessary, and in the sphere of ethics I cannot grant that objectors have established a valid position of antagonism.

Football players are young and impressionable, and every reasonable attention that can be shown them receives its reward in increased effort. A seat at the table should be used as far as possible as a reward of merit. When so recognized many players can be encouraged to stay with the game and be developed through receiving the honor of being taken to the table. The very fact of this disposition proves, on the face of it, that the man is considered worthy timber. To the young man himself, it means the inward glow of thinking that any day he may begin to realize his possibilities, become a whirlwind, and win his letter as well as fame. Again, the grind of the football season at the two-thirds stage is monotonous and severe. To take a few players from the scrub to the training table is one very encouraging and stimulating method of tiding over this vicious spot in the season.

And because everything in reason should be done at all times to brighten the mental outlook of the football player, to keep him serene of spirit, of better cheer than before, so the training table furnishes the coach with an important means of affording contrast and entertainment, and of placing men in a helpful environment.

As a means of physical improvement, the training table gives the players a chance to live differently, and to live rather better than they would be apt to do ordinarily. Boarding and fraternity houses in college towns undoubtedly provide too much pastry, pudding sauces and gravies, too much tea and coffee and too much fried food for the best interests of the undergraduate stomach. It is true that the football player could digest these dainties with less actual injury than the non-athletic student, but as the object of training is to make the player as superior as possible, he should be required to abstain from eating anything which could fail to benefit him. There is a certain thrill which accompanies denial, and the football man who is put on the table, and is thereby impressed with the fact that his eating and drinking is regarded as specially important, feels at once that it is almost an honor to be asked to abstain from eating and drinking certain things.

Training table, however, need not exclude all of the small pleasures of life with iron rigidity. Strict avoidance of tea and coffee is not essential or even advisable. These luxuries, served out with judgment as special boons, give the men greater contentment. Tea and coffee in excess are undoubtedly injurious, but the damage they do is after all slight compared, for instance, with milk, when this food, as at nearly every training table, is indulged in without restraint. Many of the strongest athletes have seriously injured themselves for the work in hand on the assumption that it is impossible to drink too much milk. One great tackle, selected by Walter Camp and a host of other experts for their "all" teams, drank so much milk before this peculiarity of his appetite was discovered and checked that he induced an internal condition strikingly suggestive of fatty degeneration. A fifty-yard sprint left him gasping and breathless. Some men, as a matter of fact, cannot drink milk at all without being injured for athletics. A quart of milk a day is sufficient for almost any athlete.

As for cream, nothing makes a man more logy. One can almost feel it choking his wind as it slides deliciously down the throat in its happy environment of strawberries or peaches. Milk, rather than cream, should by all means be served with cereals at a training table, and used, too, with the hot beverages permitted. Table water should be cooled in glass jars in the refrigerator, but not served with ice. The men should be discouraged from drinking while eating. Before and after the meal a glass of water is sufficient. While no serious harm may result from the moderate use of water during meals, the arguments against the practice are sufficiently strong to govern the man who is striving for the attainment of the highest form of physical excellence.

Yeast bread less than twenty-four hours old should not be eaten by anybody, unless thoroughly toasted. Toast is occasionally somewhat constipating, and stale bread is the preferable food for athletes. Whole wheat, rye, barley and oatmeal breads are all more nourishing than white. The bread supply should be carefully selected. It is very important that this be done. Ordinary baker's bread is not good enough.

The training table should supply all the vegetables, excepting turnips, carefully cooked and properly served. Vegetables should feature especially at the evening meal, when by their use the men may avoid the error of consuming too much meat. Men can digest more meat during the football season than at other times, but they will be better off if they consume comparatively small quantities of it at the evening meal. However, the backbone of the training table is its liberal supply of high-grade lamb and beef, chops and steaks. Eggs are a staple, too. Fresh fish, poultry, bacon, and occasionally ham, should be included for the sake of variety, but not veal or pork; except that on rare occasions a man who is naturally a great pork eater may be allowed a cut of good pork as a special boon, to encourage him in the belief that life is, after all, worth living.

It is of the utmost importance that the food shall be properly cooked and brought to table, which means, among other things, that the players must be prompt in their attendance at meals, so that courses may be served in digestible condition. Potatoes and eggs should not be fried in heavy grease. Thick soups are to be avoided, and thin soups should be skimmed repeatedly before they appear on the table. Butter, like cream, is a thing to be used sparingly by athletes. Baked beans should be thoroughly cooked. When they are thoroughly cooked, they become one of the most strengthening articles of diet that an athlete can select.

The supply of fresh and cooked fruit should be as abundant as possible. Prunes are not to be disdained, by any means, and among the fresh fruits only bananas need to be regarded with the slightest suspicion. Home-made jam, jelly and marmalade give variety to the bill of fare. Potatoes are to be avoided if fried, and also when reduction of weight has become imperative. All kinds of boiled greens are desirable. Griddle cakes in the morning need not horrify a sensible trainer. The men can digest them without injury. The great danger from griddle cakes is found in the syrups which usually accompany them. Served with a little butter and sugar, the damage they do is negligible.

For desserts, puddings and fruit salads are safest things to offer. As a general rule, the ban on pie and other lard-made pastry should very seldom be lifted. Plain cake, however, follows only the rule for bread; when new made it is unfit for consumption. Many trainers will serve cottage pudding whose hands go up in horror at the mention of cake. Cottage pudding plainly implies cake, and the material used in this confection should stand at least twenty-four hours after the original baking. Indian pudding, bread pudding, com starch, tapioca, rice and custards are recommended, and ice cream may be served occasionally for variety. Nuts and raisins also provide a welcome relief in the dreary wilderness of puddings.

Players and others should avoid overindulgence in salt. Often, through a misconception of its use, or through appetite, men use salt to a degree which thickens the blood, to the ultimate destruction of health. ·

A trainer should study individual peculiarities and tastes in the matter of diet for just such individual excesses as overindulgence in salt or milk. Athletes, moreover, are apt to be high strung, nervous, and at times irritable. Well kept, cleanly, airy, sunny eating rooms will offend nobody; while, on the other hand, many a young man reared in an atmosphere of refinement has become disgusted and nauseated by the slap-dash service and stained tablecloth of the average training table. The linen should be white, the glass and silver polished until they shine.

The seating arrangement at table should be capable of such readjustment as will remove a sensitive man from the immediate neighborhood of one whose taste in wit and humor, or whose audible method of attacking soup, is plainly causing discomfort and loss of appetite.

Break up cliques and fraternity groups. For the time being the greatest frat in college is the squad.

The trainer, presiding at table as he does, can also see to it that enough conversation and discipline is maintained to counteract the American tendency to strive for records in speed while acquiring the necessary amount of nourishment. On the walls may well hang at least one picture of a cow, an animal whose thoroughness in the matter of mastication of food offers an example singularly worthy of imitation during the football season. Arrange, if possible, the table in the form of a square or circle, with the sitters facing inward, both for sociability's sake and in order that their appetite and contentment, or the lack of either, can be readily noted by the presiding officers.

Avoid serious football talk, for the benefit of the few who otherwise will begin immediately to play the game mentally, and bolt their food. Jokes, based on the humorous incidents of the gridiron, are allowable, but there should be nothing in the nature of serious discussion or of adverse criticism.

Without babying his men unnecessarily, the trainer decidedly should give attention to those who at certain stages of the season need pampering.

There are times when it is far better to disregard training rules and consult an individual appetite; at such a time a good cut of roast pork, with the fat trimmed off, would often do an individual far more good than harm. In a more extreme case, when a man's recorded weights show that he is inclined to get fine, it sometimes pays to dismiss him from the training table for a time, and allow him carefully cooked food of his own selection elsewhere.

The varsity captain, while properly safeguarding his official prestige, should be the chum of his men while at table. That is to say, he should be amenable to the trainer's discipline in the matter of eating and drinking.

If there is a trainer, the head coach should eat elsewhere than at the table, where a degree of familiarity obtains which would include the coach, if present, and which is too pronounced for the very best results in the handling of the men. This as a general proposition. The coach should, of course, show the utmost interest in the conduct of meals, both by occasional visits and by intelligent questioning of members of the squad.

Meals should be served at the same hour throughout the season, excepting that on the day of a game set for an earlier hour than the regular hour of practice, the lunch hour should be set back, and the quantity of food reduced. This delicate operation should be accomplished without leaving any opening through which the mental attitude of the players can be injured. The player must not be permitted to imagine that starvation may overtake him between the earlier hour of luncheon and the end of the game; nor should he be given excuse for suspecting that his bodily strength may fail him in the first quarter, because of undernourishment at noonday.

At the same time, players should be told plainly that piling the stomach with food before a game is aiding the opposition; and that the digestion is unequal, during the nervous excitement which precedes a great game, to the performance of its ordinary task. A shirred egg with toast and tea is an entirely adequate luncheon for a player who is going into a championship game, and if the game is to begin at two o'clock the men should sit at table not later than eleven forty-five in the morning. At least two hours should always elapse between the end of a meal and the beginning of any period of severe physical exercise.

While outwardly belittling all injuries, the trainer and his assistants in reality will keep sharp eyes open for the merest scratches. The smallest cut may become infected and cause serious loss of efficiency. They must also look out for incipient boils, avoiding the use of poultices, which relieve one infection while spreading it to surrounding healthy tissue. Boils should be cut through with the proper surgical instrument in competent hands, and the infected area thoroughly washed out with solutions of alcohol or iodine.

Cuts in safe places should be left open to the air and sunlight, but they must usually be covered for protection, and frequent attention must be given to the processes going on beneath the bandage.

The doctor or doctors who cooperate with the football department, and to whom should be reserved the treatment of all fractures, actual or suspected, ought to work along the same lines as the coach and trainer. The doctor should not go into too much detail in informing a player of the nature of minor injuries, and should strive to encourage in the injured man the mental attitude which will aid him in healing his own troubles and save him, moreover, for future efficiency. If necessary, he can have the player laid off, without going too deeply into the nomenclature of his specific injury.

Both physician and trainer, when any of the authority is delegated to them, should use it for the good of the coach, who, in using properly his own authority for the good of the team, is safeguarding the interests of every member of the football department. The coach, whether he is fortunate enough to have a competent trainer or not, must know as much as a trainer about the physical and mental condition of his men. He must understand, whether the trainer does or not, that mental and physical condition go hand in hand together; that it is almost impossible to draw the line between them. With a stem sense of his responsibility for the health and well-being of the young men entrusted to his care and guidance he must learn to lose games, if necessary, by making substitutions, rather than permit a player to suffer permanent harm by playing even in the final game of his career while physically unfit. Common sense will teach the coach to avoid the error of using up in a preliminary game a player on whom reliance is placed for the championship contests.

The trainer's responsibilities are obviously heavy; but he should never be given any authority, nor should he assume any privileges, that will tend to weaken the hold of the coach on the men. If it is necessary to give the trainer the right to take men out of the game, then the trainer should never omit to give the final word to the coach, so that the players will understand that the coach is running the team.

The great difficulty in cases of divided authority comes in the fact that if one lazy man discovers a possible and likely avoidance of his tribulations through appeal to the trainer, the whole squad takes cognizance of this interesting condition of affairs. Nevertheless, a trainer who goes on the field to consider an injured man unquestionably should be in a position to take the man out of the game, if necessary. But coach and trainer should have a common knowledge of the men who compose the machine. They should know the reliables as well as the fakers. The trainer should know when he sees a man stretched out on the field of play the probabilities of his being really injured, and that he and the coach understand the man in the same way. If in doubt, he should remove the supposedly injured man; but he should make no haphazard guesses that will tend to injure the *esprit de corps*. He should make no remarks as to the injury of the player, remembering that he is treating one man and not the squad; remembering also that unnecessary condolences and learned disquisitions on an injury may seriously affect the player's mental condition, present and future, and his recovery. A trainer, in removing an injured player from the field, may lose the game by a remark which fills the listening players with undue fear or gives them a mental shock sufficient to undermine their wholehearted effort. It takes eleven men to play the game, and one or two men, physically perfect but mentally affected, are often difficult to discover from the sidelines although at the same time they may be actually so inefficient as to ruin teamwork and success. Finally, the trainer should never attempt to convince the players that he is a football coach, whatever his merits in that direction may actually be. He should regard himself rather as the right arm of the coach, and their mystical union should be a very real one in point of actual fact.

It is especially essential that the coach understand the desirability of developing his team with the least possible amount of scrimmage. Better an underscrimmaged than an overscrimmaged team. One of the best teams ever known to the writer had but one short scrimmage of five minutes' duration, and that only to perfect a new play, during the last five and a half weeks of the season. To be sure, this unusual lack of scrimmage work was due to a decision that the substitute material was especially weak; so that although much attention was paid to scrimmaging the substitutes, to develop them, the varsity team proper was not scrimmaged during the period mentioned. No coach should order scrimmage without careful planning of its object, or allow scrimmage to start without deciding as to its approximate length. He should inform his trainer or other assistant and be notified frequently of the flight of time. He will require such notification because, as it is impossible for a coach to attain success without enthusiasm, so it is impossible for an enthusiastic coach to realize the speedy passage of time during scrimmage. He must have some one to serve the useful purpose of an alarm clock, or he will attempt to make all of his corrections in one day. Young men are very strong, but young men overworked are very weak, and a man abused even at his favorite pastime will lose interest. And it is much easier to lose interest than to revive it.

Handling and playing with a football under the right conditions before school or college begins give a candidate a flying start. The average young man takes a certain amount of exercise during the summer as a preparation for football. Tennis and baseball, not indulged in to excess, afford as natural a preparation as any; while golf, walking and riding are excellent. Yachting and motor car driving have no preparatory value. Swimming fails to develop successful land muscles.

There have been several examples of seashore lifeguards who have found it difficult to get into shape for football, and who have proved to be comparatively short of wind, less responsive of muscle, and more lacking in stamina. In fact, it is quite possible to overestimate the value of bathing and swimming in the life of an athlete. The temporary glow and exhilaration which follows a bath is inevitably followed by a reaction, and unquestionably too much bathing lowers the vitality and resistance. After hard work it is essential that a man cleanse his body, using cool to cold water, however; as warm water is particularly weakening. The exposure to water should be as brief as consistent with cleanliness.

A football player should endeavor to get as clean as he can on the least possible quantity of water after practice, and to let the rest of the water alone as completely as possible during the remainder of the day; remembering that luxury and football do not go together.

If a man can keep clean by the one bath which he takes after practice, he should not take any more. The cold shower at night before retiring, which many young collegians seem, for various reasons, to regard as essential, should be avoided. Properly instructed youths know nowadays that nocturnal emissions, if not abnormally frequent, are entirely natural, carry no injurious consequences and afford no occasion for alarm. The young man who has been so instructed and who attaches no importance to natural incidents is under no danger that his uninstructed fears might become a reality.

Players who go under the shower daily should note the percentage of bald major leaguers in baseball, and accordingly refrain from wetting the hair too often — although many men, and women, too, wet the hair every day and yet carry abundant tresses through a long lifetime. The player should start the season with a haircut, and should wear a bathing cap when he goes under the shower, unless his hair be very dirty or sweaty.

He should also be advised strongly against borrowing headgear and other protective devices worn next the skin. Seemingly healthy men have caused infections of the skin in other healthy men by exchanging headgear, especially where a tight fit is effected by the swap. Ordinary perspiration may exert an extremely irritating effect.

Prom eminent medical authority and experience coaches and trainers have found that a large majority of physical deficiencies can be cured by proper applications of hot and cold water. The general rule to follow is to use cold water for unopened wounds, such as ordinary black eyes, swollen testicles and "charley horses;" while hot water is usually applied to bleeding wounds, both to relieve pain and to promote a flow of blood sufficient to cleanse the injury and to draw out the dead and broken tissue.

"Exercise"
Bain News Service

For injuries involving ligaments, or where the swelling is severe, it is often of great value, after making use of ice bags, to apply massage, with moderate strength, in order to aid the restoration of normal circulation. Then make a second series of cold applications, and, finally, bandage the part. In obstinate cases, leave the cold packs in position. Alternating ice applications with moderate massage will relieve "charley horse" more quickly than any other treatment. Water-on-the-knee or on the elbow, readily diagnosed by the softness of the swelling occasioned, should be treated with dry heat, to cause perspiration which will draw off the water in that way and, if possible, avert the necessity of surgical intervention. Dry heat is also employed to requicken circulation in case of injury to the joints, or wherever ligaments are abundant, as the use of hot water applications may cause serious adhesions.

Players driven so hard on the football field that they are unable to study because of drowsiness, other things being equal, are getting too much work. It is a mistake to suppose that men can be kept attentive to football all the afternoon and evening and still maintain a satisfactory rating in scholarship. A boy at school or college is, or should be, there for education first, with athletics as a part and by no means the whole of the curriculum.

The question of physical condition in relation to Lord's Day observance is sometimes perplexing. It may be said that a man who undertakes a football season owes himself the duty of taking the best possible care of himself, mentally and physically. After playing a game on the Saturday, he needs some form of light exercise on Sunday, to loosen his muscles and correct slight injuries by quickening the circulation. It becomes his duty to accept the attentions of the rubbers, and it is advisable for the whole squad to take a walk in the country, at a gait as lively as the time of the season renders natural, this exercise to be followed by a short cold shower bath and a vigorous rubdown. An entire layoff from Saturday until Monday has been shown in a long series of years to be injurious. A large percentage of injuries are suffered on Monday, despite the fact that coaches never work a man that day who has even a slight injury, and hesitate to give much sudden hard work even to the men who are fit. When the muscles are stiff, the tendency to protect small bruises is all the more pronounced, and injuries occur because the man is not working in a natural position, but is contracting his muscles defensively when he should be distending them for attack.

The trainer should be assisted if not by expert masseurs at least by rubbers who can carry out the instructions of an experienced head. Little sore spots, slight wrenches and unimportant muscle bruises can be cured by one or two massage treatments. It is highly advisable from the standpoint of the athlete's peace of mind, and to preserve his enthusiasm, that he be cared for by the rubber after a scrimmage or game. After great efforts the blood settles down, as if for a rest. Fatigue toxins form, and injuries become painful. Depression of the player's spirits, just what coaches are always fighting against, occurs.

An intelligent and helpful rubber can do a great deal, incidentally, to keep a man filled with love of the game and a scorn of slight injuries; never, however, allowing him to take unnecessary or foolish chances by failing to report to the trainer a condition which appears to be serious.

A brisk rub night and morning for every football man would be ideal from the trainer's standpoint, but unfortunately there are never rubbers enough to go around. But the player's roommate, or any other friend who has the interest of the game and of the school at heart, can render very valuable service by volunteering as a rubber and submitting himself to necessary instruction in the art.

The trainer's intention must always be to send as few men as possible home from football with depressed souls. One discouraged spirit, at certain times in the season, working diligently as gloom ever does, speedily gathers other malcontents to his banner. The trainer should teach the joys and thrills of the game, and the necessity of sufficient sleep, regular hours and a system for everything. It is impossible to keep a man joyful when his bowels are on a strike. Every man should report to the trainer the failure of his bowels to operate regularly and at least once every day. A man with diarrhea should not be worked. He needs castor oil, or a dose of salts, properly administered with relation to meals, and rest. If the weather is favorable, let him be present on the field to learn what he can, but by observation and attention and not through physical effort.

Trainers should give special observation early in the season to the tall, rangy men. Four out of five of them are weak in the back and are unable to endure the gaff as well as men built closer to the ground.

CHAPTER VII: WELCOMING THE OLD GRAD

There is a much better understanding nowadays than formerly regarding the proper scope and function of graduates who revisit the campus to assist the coach and to bring back the inspiration of many hard-fought fields to the players. The graduates themselves understand that they should not and must not attempt to coach players except in the fullest accord with the central policy and plan. They do not assume to know what any man needs unless satisfied that they understand the whole system of coaching.

There was a time when zealous graduates wrought a great deal of confusion in more than one football camp. One coach who attained later to high renown, began his regime by cleaning out a whole regiment of former stars, because convinced that a complete change of system was necessary. He was resolved that henceforth his men should receive consistent coaching, directed toward predetermined objects.

It is obvious that if the ends are coached in a certain manner, the tackle play also will be entirely different from what it would be if the ends were being instructed otherwise, A volunteer graduate coach, attempting on his own responsibility to make alterations in the play of an end, without taking the head coach into his confidence, might easily disrupt teamwork; and often he did.

Veteran stars nowadays have learned sufficient self-repression, as a rule, and their attitude more nearly than formerly represents that of a dignitary on a reviewing stand. They go on the field to urge and inspire the men, congratulating them or calling them down if sure of their premises; but specific picking out of any detail that may permit of two views, and attempts at correction or advice thereon, would no longer be ventured, I believe.

There is only one way to coach; coach alone if you must; have assistants, from one to four, if you can get them, selected to cover fairly the whole game, under the style you have decided to follow, and to help develop material for future seasons. Give these assistants strict instructions that no other style is to be attempted without obtaining the sanction of the head coach. It is very pleasant, if a head coach, to be considered a fine fellow by one's assistants, but it is better to be considered a "mean cuss" than a "fine fellow," at the expense of discipline and thoroughness. One or two inexperienced assistants, who are willing to coach under instructions, are far more useful than any number of high-class and experienced aids who are jealous of their own ideas and insist upon urging them to the players in the absence of the head coach.

The return of the old, scarred veterans to the college town to help the team is a very great benefit when these ideas are as generally accepted and as acceptable as they seem to be nowadays. The inspiration to the player of a new face and an old name, at a stage of the season when time and tempers are running short, is immediate and immensely helpful. These reunions of veterans, moreover, are occasions so entirely delightful and in accord with the spirit of the sport that no one would desire to see them discontinued, and I hope that they never will be.

CHAPTER VIII: CAPTAINS AND THEIR AUTHORITY

The captain should have the authority, until he abuses it, to call for a substitute to take a man's place during a game. He can see things oftentimes that the coach from the sideline is unable to detect. But the moment abuse or favoritism steps in, this power should be taken from him. The coach can use his own method, as circumstances dictate, to communicate this change to a captain; but the captain should be spared such humiliation as might hurt his play or the confidence of the team in him. There should always be a head to any serious business. No sane, logical person could consider anyone else, except the man who has been engaged because of demonstrated ability and superior experience as the head of a football team. That man is the coach.

Like a man in business, a captain who talks too much, is seldom able to command attention. Speech making, as a habit, is to be deplored. Words of commendation or of justifiable complaint to individuals are advisable; but his address to the team as a whole, on or off the field, should be selected with the nicest discernment, used as seldom as possible, and at the psychological moment only.

By custom, at many schools, the captain is expected to talk as if he were a superior being. He should not forget that he was a private the season before, took his medicine from the coaches like the rest, and exhibited his defects to his teammates. They have thought enough of him to elect him captain, but when occasion arises they can recall his defects in seasons past very quickly, as well as his present defects. Even the soldier is human, though oftentimes his superior officer forgets it.

If a captain, as sometimes happens, is not a good mixer with his men off the field, he should, without in any way weakening his position, avoid unnecessary association with them. Here the word "unnecessary" is important. No captain should ever place himself in a position to be criticized adversely by avoiding reasonable association. Bearing in mind at such times the importance of maintaining the prestige his captaincy should give him, he must show entire readiness to meet and talk and joke with the players. In fact, so far as possible, his status as captain should disappear on these occasions, which should, however, be few.

The good mixer can afford to associate more often with his men as an equal, without weakening his prestige on the field.

The captain should take exceeding care to be in fine fettle when his season opens. He is looking disaster in the eye if he assumes the position of a guardian and overseer only; of the man who is through with the pick and shovel, but is going to tell his last year's playmates how and where to dig. To be sure, he should convince them at the beginning of the season, and maintain that position throughout, that he is their leader. But he should be able and eager to help carry the burden and to do, if anything, a little more than his share.

He should talk, and he only should talk, to the officials during the game, on most points. He should know the basis of his contention; which does not preclude his having other men on the team who also know the rules and the right or wrong of the point involved.

He should make it a rule never to interfere with the quarterback, unless fully satisfied that intervention is necessary. Even then he should not order a change in the signal unless the quarter is unable to convince him that the original signal should stand. If possible to avoid it, do not weaken the quarterback's confidence in his own good judgment.

At some colleges and schools the duties and privileges of the varsity football captain have declined and diminished to two. He runs on the field ahead of the team, carrying the ball; and he continues to hold the chief implement of the game in the group picture taken at the end of the season.

At the other extreme, where the tradition of the captain's prestige has persisted longest, is the undergraduate leader who takes advice grudgingly from the elders of the game, picks his own coach, and raises more or less doubt as to who may be the president of the college or school. Where is the reasonable mean between these two extremes?

Sound football does not admit of the election of a captain on grounds of popularity or politics. The captain should be chosen for his fighting quality and playing ability. The extraordinary power of leadership, often discovered at election time in some man who has never had actual opportunity to prove that he has it, develops too often as propaganda, indulged in by enthusiastic political groups. The biggest men on a football team in the day of battle are the men who produce results, regardless of their popularity or affiliations off the field.

Give the players the leader of their natural choice, who can be their inspiration where inspiration wins. I believe that a captain should be a senior, if a suitable man can be found in that class. It is better for the game, however, to take a junior choice, if the man has the real, big qualifications, than a senior who from all indications will not qualify. No senior worthy of his school or college will hesitate to give his best to a junior captain if the junior is a better man than he.

You are not trying to make a hit with your adversary by your choice of a captain; you are trying to make a hit with your own team, and no subterfuge should hide this truth. The captaincy is, and should be, a reward of merit; for there is no other solid basis in the showing up to that time on which to elect.

It is often debated whether the captaincy award should be so considered, or whether captains should be chosen for ideal qualities, such as a fancied ability to lead. Both points of view are harmonized when the true scrapper is chosen. Sometimes a man is found who seems to have the necessary qualifications, but who is shy in some particular, the lack of which should eliminate him from serious consideration.

The man who loses his temper will fail too often as a fighter to be placed high in that category.

The man of inferior moral standards eliminates himself likewise. The man who is merely pugnacious is not a true fighter in the football sense.

But the true scrapper is a man who contributes unbegrudgingly all that he has to the cause; not to the game or to the day, but to the team, to the whole season.

He will be a captain who feels to the fullest the importance and the responsibilities of his position. He will insist on the performance, in every detail, of all that may contribute to success. He will recognize his solemn duty to know the rules, and be able to talk earnestly and convincingly to the officials whenever the occasion arises.

No team should ever be left entirely to the devices of the captain or the quarterback. No team should be subject to the failure of the captain or quarterback. Every team should have at least five men who know the game and know the rules well; and at least two men who have the rules at their fingertips, and who can and will come to the rescue if their superiors are unable to continue in the game.

CHAPTER IX: GENERAL THEORY OF LINE DEFENSE

There are three ways to defend against closed formation plays: first, with every lineman standing up; second, with all men from tackle to tackle on the ground, charging through the spaces and converging toward a point fifteen yards beyond center; third, a combination of the foregoing styles. In the standing defense, the forward is instructed to be prepared to charge his immediate opponent by a forward leap into a position from which he cannot himself be dislodged, with one leg thrown forward, the other braced behind, and arms extended to meet the charge. He is coached to hold the opponent off until the direction of the play is properly sensed; then, if the onslaught comes his way, to fight through to it, or else use opponents' bodies and his own to block the play until help arrives from one side or the other.

The standing defense, however, permits the attack its chance to get to the line of scrimmage. This virtually invites the players on the opposite side of center to run across behind their own line and render aid. The amount of help a player can give after running across behind his own center is seldom equal to the value of the help the player originally attacked could have given himself had he charged fast into the threatened space instead of holding off his immediate opponent pending the arrival of reinforcements. The time to stop a play is when it starts. Ask any halfback whether he prefers to play against an end who waits at the line of scrimmage or against one not naturally quite so capable who rushes into the backfield!

The standing line, by its very nature and policy, is, to a certain degree, conservative from the start. Except at the tackles, it makes little attempt to get into the backfield to do things there. It calls rather for a waiting attitude, for attempts at diagnosis and for action only when action can be based on that diagnosis. When the diagnosis is incorrect the danger is grave, especially with respect to the men who have felt impelled to attempt to stop plays on the other side of the line, a brilliant performance which may even lead to an "All-America" rating if often and conspicuously repeated. Unfortunately the players who leave their positions thus are very decidedly exposing their team to return plays and delayed bucks. To be trustworthy, their power of diagnosis must be sure indeed.

"Line Defense"
National Photo Company

The standing, waiting defense enjoys the favor and approval of several of the more renowned among the big varsity coaches. It is employed by a majority, perhaps, of the big varsity teams. It is unquestionably sufficient against inferior teams, and it takes no advantage, certainly, of an equally efficient team if the latter plays the same style of defense. But for those who favor it comes the alarming sight every year of one of these standing teams, so coached, but in adversity, unable to stop the attack, suddenly throwing up the defense it has practiced all the season and assuming a lower and still lower defensive position; until finally the line is down where it belongs, on its hands, on the ground, where a man can naturally protect himself to best advantage, and making its most desperate effort in that lowly position. The sorely beset line generally manages to turn the tide back. It has been forced into the instinctive position of all lines when compelled to the conclusion that something desperate must be done in order to hold at least the ground it still can call its own.

The crouched defense, with all men from tackle to tackle on the ground and ready to spring at the first snap of the ball, is not of itself sufficient at all times. If the guards are outside the attacking guards, and if the center is charging every time, nothing can come through the middle of the line, provided the defensive quarter knows his business and will play the game. But against many forms of attack it is very essential that certain men be crouched in a sufficiently high position to be able to see what is going on behind the opponents' line. This brings us to the third method of defense, and the correct one, which assumes an extreme crouch against regular formations, and by certain men a more nearly erect position against shifts and spreads.

One marked superiority of the charge from the ground through spaces is the almost incontestable advantage that the players employing it gain from being able to observe the minutest movement of the ball and the telltale habits of the center and quarterback. The standing defense charges at best after the attacking team has started, or the fastest member of it. The crouched defense, catching the rhythm of the numbers leading up to the starting signal, and able to see the ball, is able, at least occasionally, to match the jump of the attack with a practically simultaneous charge. This defense, if there is any fair degree of equality in personnel between the two lines, will stop many more plays before they reach the scrimmage line than will the stand-up style.

Take seven men charging ferociously with the snap of the ball, regardless of where the play is going, their arms and bodies so placed that they cannot be rooted up, and no plays except center bucks can be formed well. It is called a blind charge, as each man advances with no other assumption than that he, and he alone, must stop the play; but it is very far from being a blind charge in reality. For although the head and neck are carried in stiff alignment with a straight spine, using the skull as a battering ram, the players are taught to look up through their own eyebrows as they advance and to miss no detail of information which might prove serviceable.

If there were a perfect defense there would never be any gains, and football would be dead. But I believe this defense to be theoretically correct and practically adequate.

Although the terms "offensive" and "defensive" are used herein to distinguish the team which has possession of the ball, I recognize the fact that "defensive" is an extremely unfortunate word to employ in football coaching. The psychology of the word is bad. It poisons the mental attitude of a team and robs its work of many sterling qualities. Personally I have always instructed my teams that they are on the offensive when the other team has the ball. They are not defending themselves; they are taking the ball away from the opponents.

The team imbued with the idea that it is "on the defensive" is too prone to acquire a mental attitude inferior to that of the team carrying the ball. This often very naturally develops a smug sense of defense which only too frequently comes to include a feeling of protection against injury, or prevention of long gains. This attitude once acquired by the defending team cracks the fighting spirit, and exposes the man who is trying to play football with the idea of self-protection to a greater liability to injury. Too many football players lose a certain degree of interest when not in possession of the ball. They should be taught to believe that so-called defensive play is every whit as aggressive as any actual attempt to advance the ball.

Of the five linemen from tackle to tackle I expect, then, and demand, on defense, a low crouch, hands on the ground, an immediate charge, powerful and determined, regardless of the direction of the play. The only possible exceptions, on account of the interference, oftentimes from the outside of the offensive end, or under certain conditions, to be specified later, are the tackles.

The tackles must at all times make a decisive charge without waiting for the direction of the attack; but they may, by special permission, charge from a higher position, either to improve their charge or to circumvent the opposing end.

Against the narrow side of an unbalanced line, and also, at certain times, against very wide, quick shifts, in cases where they find themselves practically doing the duty of ends, with the actual ends falling back to become secondary defense men, tackles are also permitted and even advised to charge from higher positions than the guards and center.

The defensive play of the tackle and end would be almost similar were it not that the tackle must expect considerable interference with his plans from a wily and determined offensive end. Palpably, if there were not serious interference by the offensive end with the predatory plans of an able and determined defensive tackle, there would be little need for a defensive end. The defensive end, as a rule, encounters no immediate opposition, and his charge may be made from a less extreme crouched position than the other forwards must adopt.

The unbalanced attacking formation, sometimes called tackle over, generally results from shifts, and when completed leaves four men on one side of center and two on the other. From this formation it is to be assumed that at least sixty per cent of the plays will go to the strong side, although there should be, and generally are, very effective and dangerous plays which go to the short side. This is typically a running attack formation. The defensive tackle on the short side should stand up. He must be ready to make a stiff charge, with his arms in front, in order to meet the periodical attack and to assure himself that he will not be blocked by the attacking end on the same side. Against a balanced formation, however, both tackles should be down on the ground.

If the attacking quarterback now leaves his position, one center trio man at once becomes a second defensive quarterback, except on kick formations, when a kick is assured; but ordinarily one should never trust to a six-man line, unless for some specific game or for some special reason. At best the loose center foregoes the advantage of being able to give the snapper-back that direct shock every two or three plays which wears the latter out so rapidly, and makes his job so difficult. As a general proposition the center's place is on the line where he can continually worry and tire the opposing center, disturb the quarterback, and stop plays directed through the middle.

The low defense, with a sprinting charge directed at spaces rather than at opponents, is immeasurably the better against a normal line. Even when the men stand and spread against shift plays in order that they can close in more readily to meet the shift, linemen do not use their hands and arms as in the standing defense; but take their new positions quickly for a blind charge. The attacking line, unsteady after making its jump, is bound to be upset somewhat by a driving charge. The defensive charge continues to be a blind charge, for the reason that every man must assume that the play is coming at him.

CHAPTER X: DEFENSE AGAINST SHIFTS AND SPREADS

Defense against the regular formation, balanced line, where one man is called over to the other side to make a four and two combination, generally calls for only a slight modification. There is usually no haste or deception involved, and the defense man can shift as quickly as his enemy. The tackle on the narrow side generally assumes a standing position. He takes the same relative position to the attacking end as before, if the end is playing moderately close to the next inside man. If unable to drive through the end, to prevent his going down under forward passes, the tackle's next thought is for check plays, crisscrosses and quarterback runs to the short side.

The next man inside tackle assumes a position opposite the quarterback, if the. latter is standing on either side of center. If the quarter is directly behind center, however, he charges the guard hole nearest his tackle on the short side. He and all the remaining line play the straight, low charging, defensive game, fighting to the play after the initial charge. This last statement means that they can at least give support to the defensive man on either side.

The next phase is the unexpected sudden shift of the line to left or right. Plainly there is no opportunity to send men over to either side to balance the shift. Here the opponents are depending upon speed in the shift and the immediate charge to take advantage of weakness. This calls for a slide of the defensive line to the side toward which the shift has been made, merely balancing the line as before. If the defensive team keeps cool, there is no fundamental reason for finding itself under any disadvantage. The quick shift of a line with a play immediately ensuing has a strong tendency to weaken the charge, which offsets what would otherwise be a considerable advantage.

Here again the tackle on the deserted side plays the standing defense. The secondary defense merely moves over into a position of balance.

Now we come to the more important and dangerous shifts. They are only dangerous, however, when the defensive team has not been coached soundly on the principles of defense against fast shifting offense. Let us take the best-known shifts of this kind, where the center alone remains upon the line, or the center and two guards, or perhaps the center and the two ends playing wide. The rest of the team retires to a formation in the backfield from which at a given signal it can quickly adjust itself into a legal formation and get away at once with its play.

There are two things now which must be done by the defense as soon as opponents are called into the backfield to take their positions. First the tackles and ends must be spread to be in the strongest possible defensive position for the widest close-formation line possible; that is to say, five men on one side of center and one on the other. Therefore each tackle, assuming that five men are to pile on his side of center, should be outside the next to the last man, and practically opposite the last man, presumably an end, unless this last man leaves a large space between his presumable tackle and himself.

In this case the defensive tackle assumes a position just outside the offensive tackle, driving behind the opponents' line of scrimmage at all costs, and taking special care not to be blocked by the offensive end.

The second necessary preparation is to bring back one of the center trio, the best man for the purpose, placing him four yards behind the line of scrimmage in a position between his defensive guard and tackle as they would be in regular formation. The defensive quarter assumes a corresponding position on the other side of center. Each remaining center trio man assumes a position halfway between the ball and his own tackle. All are standing as high as necessary to observe at the first possible moment the extent of the shift. The moment this is ascertained the defensive shift is made accordingly.

If the worst that can happen to a line that was unprepared does happen, to wit, a five-man jump to one side of center, the tackle on the strong side immediately drops to the ground, preparatory and all set for an immediate charge against a line that is wobbly. The end also is in a state of preparedness. The defensive guard on the side of the shift has only a slight readjustment to make. He jumps over one man and makes his charge between the twin tackles and the twin guards. The guard on the weak side slides rapidly to a position opposite but slightly outside the offensive guard next to center on the strong side. The tackle on the weak side slides to a position slightly outside the one forward, probably an end, on his side of center, to charge against him and toward the quarter, guarding especially against any quarterback nm. The end on the weak side comes in halfway toward center, to charge into the backfield, watching for crisscrosses and chasing the play.

The two defensive quarterbacks have shifted immediately with the strength of the play. The quarter who found himself nearest to the short side of the line crosses slightly to the other side of opponents' center, keeping an eye on the offensive quarterback until the latter has moved away from center or until the ball has been passed. The other defensive quarter stands behind and just inside his own tackle. The two defensive quarterbacks are used in this case plainly because of their excellent power of observation from this position, their increased defensive strength due to the lost power of charge by the line which has just shifted, and as an insurance against any faulty shifting of their own line.

The two defensive halfbacks balance their own line.

If the shift develops into a four and two line, the defensive tackle on the strong side slides in the distance of one space. The guard is already set. He charges the second space from center. The guard on the weak side shifts to a position between guard and center on his side. He charges toward and through center, to prevent quarterback plunges and to defend against center bucks. The tackle on the weak side charges through the outside man. The defensive quarterbacks assume corresponding positions four yards from the line of scrimmage, balancing the line as before. So, too, the defensive halfbacks stand as usual eight yards from the line of scrimmage.

Strange to say, the most disconcerting shift after the with-drawal of most of the offensive team into the backfield is the sudden return to an evenly balanced line. As the line and backs make their jump there are sufficient numbers leaping to either side to confuse slightly the defensive line as to its own immediate moves. Both tackles are inclined to believe that the power of the shift is coming to their side. The guards may also be deceived, and fail to shift sufficiently, or with sufficient speed, or both. The result is that wide gaps are left in the line. The principal idea in meeting quick shifts is to place tackles and ends in the most effective positions possible before knowledge can be had of the exact proportions of the shift. A defensive team is in a better po-sition if caught by the snap of the ball sliding toward center than sliding away from center. As the chief purpose of quick shifts is to develop a method of rounding the tackles, the safest basis to start from is to locate the tackles before the shift in positions where they can thwart that intention.

There are thousands of plays from very widely spread formations. The same general system of defense holds against all of them. In practically all cases most of the defensive line is standing. The only important exception to a standing line defense under these conditions is where four or five attacking forwards including center remain in closed formation, with the quarterback under center. If this number is sufficient to warrant the defense of three linemen, one man should be playing on the ground, opposite the quarterback. If the quarter is directly behind and facing center, this defender should charge through the center rush toward the strength of the opponents' line.

Naturally, with a line decidedly spread, it is essential that a defensive line should see what is going on. It is also essential that the enemy's strength or weakness be taken in at a glance. It is important to note whether the backfield remains intact or not. If the backfield is spread considerably, its power of running attack is much reduced. Therefore, beyond careful defense around center, there is little cause for balancing the opposing line with defensive linemen. Perhaps four or five linemen should be used, not too far from the ball, in order to circumvent any wild attempt by the opponents. But against such formations it is seldom necessary to maintain more than five men on the line. The more plainly it is shown that the formation is distinctly a forward-passing one, the more surely should the defensive strength against the passing game be augmented. Keep firmly in mind this special rule. Always balance the offensive team, not the offensive line, nor the offensive backfield.

A good example is the defense on a formation in which two or three men are sent out to one side, fifteen to twenty yards away from the rest of the team. If these two or three men are backs, the running attack of the team is practically ruined. If two of these men, for example, happen to be a tackle or guard and an end, it will be seen at once that one of the defensive linemen can be spared from the line. The tackle or end on the weakened side can be dropped back into the defensive halfback's position on that side. The halfback, so relieved, can take a deep position, in a line with the far-flung squadron sent to the side of the field for the ostensible purpose of receiving a forward pass. If he plays twenty yards deep, the teams are now well balanced. The linemen who took the defensive halfback's position can back up the line if necessary, though two linemen are gone, and can also be effective against forward passes in the territory halfway between his position and that of the halfback who is playing deep.

Many teams are needlessly unnerved by the appearance of two or three opponents in a distant position, and feel that they must match them man for man. They fail to grasp two ideas: first, this forward pass will be hurried by the defensive men on the wings; second, only one ball will be thrown, and defensive players must of necessity, in case of long passes, play the ball in total disregard of the men. In short, remember that a guard, tackle and end without a full line are superfluous; and one of them, at least, is in his wrong position. Therefore, if the offensive savors of a forward pass, one of these men should be in his own backfield, to prevent its consummation. Do not forget that your wingmen, whether guards, tackles or ends, are charging into the backfield immediately, to break up plays before they are formed and to hurry or block forward passes or kicks.

CHAPTER XI: SECONDARY DEFENSE

The defensive quarter, in normal defensive alignment, plays four yards behind the center. The halfbacks play eight yards behind and slightly outside of the ends, who are playing eight feet from their tackles. The defensive quarter is really the backbone of the defense. He should be heavy and powerful, but above all he must be a man of rare judgment and quick decision. He is directly responsible for practically all long gains. He must stop line bucks, outside tackle plays and end runs; he must defend against short forward passes from one end of the line to the other. A willing worker with great ability in this position offsets a mediocre rushline. But the best lines are not strong enough without a good defensive quarter.

The primary rule for the secondary defense is to keep all eyes on center; then quarterback, if he is playing under center; then ends. A secondary defense man with his eyes on center cannot fail to see the quarterback and both ends. If the quarterback does not leave center there is cause for uneasiness by the defensive quarterback, unless he can see the ball go. Unless the ball goes the quarterback has it. The two defensive halfbacks must watch the same thing, because the defensive quarterback might not. Defensive backs also get the story immediately if the ends are coming down the field. It is not sufficient for the left halfback to center his attention on his opponents' right end. The enemy may have planned to surprise and deceive by sending the other end diagonally across the field, to take a long forward pass behind the position which the halfback has failed to guard. The halfbacks, as well as the defensive quarter, have a very difficult task, which necessitates quick judgment and intelligence; but these things, the movement of the ball from center, its pass, and the charge of the ends, are all observed in a moment, and all three men must be in preparatory positions for speed as the ball is snapped. Their charge into the defense must be very fast, but the observation of these especially important matters will not perceptibly impede their motion.

There is another very important thing to look for which only occurs occasionally but is dangerous to overlook. That is the running back by the man in possession of the ball, or one not in possession of it, into a receiving position. The discovery of this movement in time may be the means of preventing a very successful forward pass. I have always called the defensive halfback on the side away from the play "the conservative back." He is secondarily responsible for crisscrosses or delayed bucks on his side of the line. He is the only man left to defend his entire side of the field against a diagonally thrown forward pass, cleverly contrived for use when the attack has started in the other direction and when everything looks particularly safe so far as he is concerned. This does not mean that he should not and does not figure against plays on the other side of the line, especially if they are wide and have gained some ground. He merely waits until he has seen the run started, with the crisscross possibility eliminated, and until assured that neither end is charging in his direction. Furthermore, he must be especially sensitive to the merest suggestion that either end is slipping into the territory that the defensive quarter has left unprotected; for the defensive quarter, having seen the ball passed, or the quarterback running from behind center, presumably with the ball, is justified in rushing to the point of probable attack. So, also, is the other defensive halfback justified, having seen no evidence of a forward pass into his zone. Therefore this third and last, close secondary defense man must defend the region that the defensive quarterback has left.

For the treatment of the immediate secondary defense I have purposely omitted from this discussion the defensive fullback, who is, all this time, playing twenty-five yards from the line of scrimmage, and, like all the others, counting the down and, so far as possible, the distance to be gained. He is standing in a position where he can best take part in whatever may happen on either side, and therefore with a tendency toward the center of the field as regards the sidelines, even when the teams are playing close to the sidelines. He should observe carefully every injunction that is put upon the three other backs. Judging by results, there are very few defensive fullbacks who would qualify along these lines. It is a very common sight to see a back or an end outstripping this last and final defender of the goal line. It seems almost incredible that he should not at least get a chance to tackle the runner, if he has kept his eyes and his ears open.

CHAPTER XII: CENTERS AND THE SPIRAL PASS

Weight and height, within reasonable limits, are of no particular significance in selecting a center. Among the best centers I have seen there was one whose average weight for the season was one hundred fifty pounds, and another who tipped the beam regularly at two hundred twelve pounds. Candidly, I have a slight preference for the two hundred twelve pounder, not only for the mental effect of his bulk on the other team, but also because he naturally did have more effectiveness than the lighter man. My main point, however, is that not all is lost because the center rush is a light man.

The light man must have plenty of fight, be a good diagnostician of plays, and possess a little extra speed to make up for the driving power and the defensive power of many more pounds of good flesh and muscle generally presumed to be necessary in a center.

In picking your snapper-back, take the man with plenty of fight, nerve and stamina. In a pinch, the man with plenty of fight can be substituted, in choosing, for the man with stamina. Most men have enough of the latter at the end of the season, if they have the willingness to use it. Always bear in mind that a center has a big task on his hands, and is veritably the hub of the wheel. Discourage him, and the offensive power of the team disappears.

He seldom is given the credit he deserves. Most followers of the game assume a good center as a matter of course, knowing little of the hardships he must endure. He must be able to with-stand all efforts to intimidate or to infuriate him. He must be willing and ready to take a bad drubbing, while in a position in which he has little opportunity to defend himself. He must pass, pass, pass, all the time, and ceaselessly practice the most natural position from which to acquire a powerful charge simultaneously with the pass. He must make all his passes from the same initial position, if he is to mask the play of his team. He must be able not only to do this, but to do it so naturally that his charge is very little weakened, if any, by his pass or by his extra duties.

Naturally, then, all offensive play starting with the center (or a man who takes his place on a shift, thereby becoming a center) the caliber of his work becomes the first consideration and a very weighty one. He must weather continual abuse and withstand a thousand efforts to "get his goat" in practice, or it is doubtful if he will be able to maintain his standard of passing when put to those tests in a game.

The center, standing on his own ten-yard line, with his team all set for a punt, suggests the baseball pitcher with bases full and three balls and no strikes on the batter. Like the pitcher, the center stands alone, almost everything depends upon that pass, and no little attention which can legally be offered to make him fail will be omitted by the opposing team. It is indeed a tense moment, and his hand and his heart must be right. Think this over when you are picking your center. He may not have all the necessary qualifications when you pick him; but consider he is competent to rise to the standard. The center needs friends on a team; needs guards who show confidence in him; a quarterback who is with him heart and soul; a punter who believes in him.

At the same time, give me the little one hundred fifty-pound center whom I once saw on his own one-foot mark, with his team lined up for a kick. He turned around to his punter before get-ting down on the ball, and made him a little speech. He insisted, among other things, in no uncertain tones, that he and his team mates now had the opposition at a tremendous advantage; and that, with the protection of the backs, the kicker was bound to boot the ball at least fifty yards. There is a center rush for you! If you have a man like him on your squad, let him manage the ball.

Assuming that the quarterback is up under the center, the ball is passed so that the end of the egg goes into a cup formed by the heels of the former's hands and completed by his extended fingers as they tighten on the ball, with the tips at or near its middle. The quarter's fingertips are four inches from the near end of the ball when he is set to receive the pass.

Nothing but absolute abandonment of the ball by the center can make it do anything but fit into the cup. The fumble of a dry ball, in case of doubt, should be attributed to the failure of the center. Nine times out of ten it is his fault.

Centers should learn and practice two passes: the spiral, and the pass which may be termed regular. The spiral is much the faster and better pass; and as the handing of the ball to the quarterback can be accomplished just as well without changing the position of the hands, the spiral would be the only pass to learn if it could be used with a mud-covered ball. As a mud-covered ball is sometimes inevitable, centers must also be able to use the slower pass. They are at no particular disadvantage in this case, as the same mud retards charging and blocking rather more than it retards the speed of the passing for kicks.

The ball is usually passed to the quarterback with the center's hands in the position used in making the long, regular pass. If, then, the spiral pass, involving a different position of the hands on the ball, were used exclusively for passing to the last man in the backfield on kick formations, too much advance information would be afforded the defense. A team should have and should use, if only for deception, plays in which the ball is passed direct to members of the backfield other than the quarter and the man in punting position; and on these plays the center should pass in the same manner as for the kick, pass or run resulting from passes to the fullback.

It is also well for the center to mix up his passes to the quarterback, using the two styles alternately, even should he have a slight preference for the "regular" style in feeding the ball to his field general. This is especially true if the quarterback stays under center until the ball is passed for kicks or direct to backs other than the kicker. If the center uses his "regular" pass for the handling of the ball through the quarterback, but goes to the spiral when he intends to throw deep, the effect of the quarterback's deception, involved in his presence under center, is entirely lost. Therefore, when the spiral is used at all, many of the center's short passes to his quarterback should be made on the spiral plan.

When he is in position to make the "regular" pass, the center's hands should be placed in corresponding positions, one on each side of the ball and slightly in advance of its middle as it lies at right angles to the lines of scrimmage; the fingertips touching the ground, the thumbs forward and almost meeting on top of the ball as they converge toward each other. The ball is thrown or passed with one continuous motion.

The long pass is really an arm throw, with no snap of the wrists, the elbows being held stiff. The arms "follow through" until stopped by the contact of the elbows with the legs.

The position of the hands is a little different for the spiral pass. Here the right hand is held in advance of the left, and in a lower position. The left thumb and its heel bear down on top of the ball, with the thumb at its center. The right hand, two inches farther forward on the ball than the left, is tucked as far underneath as the rules allow, the fingers touching the ground. The pass is made like the longer "regular" pass, bearing in mind the small pressure exerted by the left thumb. The arms "follow through" and are stopped by the thighs as in the other long pass. The natural inclination of the arms and shoulders is to readjust themselves and to go through between the legs equally. There is a slight sensation of twisting the ball as this readjustment is made. When it is completed, and the ball is leaving the hands, the left hand will have dropped and the right been brought up, sufficiently so that both are equidistant from the ground. The elbows land on the legs as in the other long pass.

The spiral is faster than the "regular" pass because the right hand slams the ball through with some resenting pressure from the left, and this quiet resistance gives the right hand more of a chance to follow through. The pass is a great deal like a throw, and the proof of this assertion is that a left-handed center insists on placing his left hand forward on the ball, rather than his right.

The spiral is also a more accurate pass than any other. A good spiral passer will look at his man and figure his distance before making his pass. After that he may or may not give a backward glance between his legs as the ball goes. He seems to be able to direct the ball while giving most of his attention to his own charge.

It is by far the best pass for punters to handle. It comes to the kicker end first, and is very easy to catch. It wedges itself into the hands in the simplest possible position to adjust for kicking. The kicker has nothing to adjust, in fact, except to turn the ball lacing up. The pass is only impossible with a muddy ball, when all passing is likely to be poor. It is not bad in merely wet weather.

Next to fast charging ends, the fast-charging defensive center is the most disconcerting customer. Prom his place on the line, or very close to it, let him crash into his immediate opponent the very first time the latter handles the ball, and on the next lineup, let him repeat the lesson. The snapper-back not only becomes worried about his passing, but the ambition of the quarterback to cut through the middle of the line with the ball is sensibly diminished.

On the next down, if the quarterback is standing sideways, the defensive center may vary his charge by crowding himself into the opposite space between center and guard, having all due understanding of the number of the down and the distance to be gained.

He will not omit to jar the snapper-back once more as he charges, but this time the object of his attack is to expose the quarterback and to test as quickly as possible the latter's nerve and steadiness under fire. However, by crowding against the center rather than against the guard, as he goes through, he will tend to block up the opposite guard hole as well as the one he has invaded; besides slowing up the center's charge and otherwise annoying him.

CHAPTER XIII: QUARTERBACK PLAY

In picking quarterbacks my first inclination would be for a man of strong, magnetic voice, confident manner, and pronounced natural activity. No doubt this idea may be considered surprising, the general impression being that the first requisite of a good quarterback is brains. I appreciate brains in a quarterback, if they are possible to be had; but I shall not alter my list of qualifications in point of importance. However, if the man lacks any of the above qualifications, including brains, he cannot be my quarterback, unless he is the best of a bad lot. When so unfortunate as to have a quarterback of inferior mental caliber, I give him a cardinal rule to follow. That rule is: "When in doubt, kick the ball."

It must be admitted that the youngster who impresses a coach as being good timber for quarterback may seldom be accused of excessive diffidence regarding his own abilities and possibilities, such as they are. A certain amount of egotism may be apparent and pardonable in him. It may even be intimated by his critics occasionally that the young man exhibits a barely perceptible tendency toward a swelled head. As he will have to calculate chances and make radical decisions under fire on the football field, it is quite as well that at least the dominant note of his character shall not be a profound distrust of his own judgment. His self-confidence, unless it be actual folly, is one of the last things that will die in him and it is generally backed up by courage. Probably it is based on successful participation and leadership in various youthful activities, and a certain demonstrated ability to hold his own among the small intrigues and feuds of boyhood. All his life he has loved to take chances, but he has also learned the importance of calculating those chances before making his choices. He may cherish in secret a world of confidence in his own "hunches," in his lucky star, in some mystic gift of decision; a faith never shaken by serious failure. But, even so, his hunches generally are based on sound, instinctive judgment and a keen sense of reality. In any event, his ability to do the right thing at the right time has already won the decided toleration of his elders and the respectful admiration of his own "gang." He is considered good company, because he has shown that he can take care of himself. His popularity rests on the solid esteem which boys always accord to the fellow who shows courage, daring, and the ability to do well the things that bigger lads are doing.

All these qualities are expressed and indicated, somehow, in the swagger, ever so slight, of his walk; in the clear light of his eyes; in the confident and undefeated timbre of his voice. You pick him, as I have said, on generalities, but the signs seldom fail. Quarterbacks are born and not made, and it is seldom indeed that a fairly experienced eye can discover no outward sign of a spiritual heritage. There is something about this youngster, chosen for his voice, for his abundant nervous energy and for intelligent eyes, with a smoldering fire behind them, that rarely misleads his sponsor. There is something about him, too, which his opponents on the football field will be equally certain to recognize as the embodiment of moral force, potent for their undoing unless they can match it with something finer. He will be able to intimidate them with that voice, unless they can show themselves men indeed and weaklings in no wise.

It must be part of his reputation and part of his quality to be ever so fair, as manly boys go. He is rather above petty likes and dislikes, rather superior to all small politics. The best play for the given situation always, — that will be his rule of conduct as a quarterback both before and after he becomes famous. Other things being equal, he will give every back, regular and substitute, a fair share of the work and of the honors, too. Disdain to play favorites will apply to everybody, his own roommate included, and when sacrifice is demanded he will be the last to spare himself. Boys and men alike are always delighted to follow this sort of leadership. They will stand any amount of driving, or urging, if not accompanied by abuse, when convinced that it is intended for the good of the team.

Like other great leaders, our potential quarterback will not always share his mental reasoning with those around him, nor reveal his whole intention to them; but he can count usually on enthusiastic agreement and admiring acquiescence when he finally gives the word and points the way. When, on the twenty-five-yard line, with five minutes to play, our quarterback says to himself: "I've got a chance to tie. I've got a good drop-kicker. We are in front of the posts. The wind is not bad. But I'll not try it. I don't want a tie. I want to win. A touchdown will do it. It's up to me to put it over" — and he barks out the signal for a forward pass or a running play, the dullest member of the eleven understands, and the least daring sets himself with fiery resolution for the charge, both glad in their hearts that the more courageous choice has been made.

The same quarterback, backed up to his own twenty-yard line, will hold another little argument with himself; although the mental process will be over and completed in a lightning flash. Put into words, his reasoning might take this form: "According to zone play, I ought to kick. We are all set for a kick and so are they. The other team expects it. If we kick we shall be lucky to stop the runback short of the forty-five-yard line. When it's all over they will boot the ball back, and our position won't be a bit better than it is now. The great, big gamble here is to get away! If I throw a long forward pass, such as we have, there is a mighty good chance for us to recover it. But if we don't, they can't get it. Even if they should, our whole line will be down there. They wouldn't be able to run the ball back any farther than they might be able to run back a kick. In fact, they wouldn't have as good a chance. I've also got a trick play with very little danger in it of a fumble. It ought to work. It will catch them off their guard. We must get ourselves out of this hole. I've picked my play now, and I'm going to try it!"

His plays and signals, to the minutest detail, the quarterback must know without mental effort. Upon the discovery of a weakness he should never have to think, "What play have I that goes there?" Rather should he say, "Now for 72." He must know his position on the field as a child knows the way to the doughnut pail. It should never be necessary for him to waste any time finding out whether he is on his own twenty-five-yard line or the opposing team's forty.

Every member of a good football team, but more particularly the quarterback, must early acquire the habit of knowing the down and the approximate distance to be gained. There is no excuse for the execution of a ridiculous play on the fourth down, or on any other down, merely because the quarterback has a temporary fit of mental aberration. A captain should instinctively discover the error at once, and so should every other member of the team.

This, however, does not mean that ten men should immediately attempt to cram intellect into the poor quarterback's dome. Nor does it mean that even the captain should be perpetually attempting to prove to the quarterback, to the coach, or to himself, the error of his general's judgment. The captain, on the field, is G. H. Q.; not the general. He should know fully the plan and command the game as a whole; should lend immediate assistance when the general is in a serious dilemma; but the general, so long as there is a chance of his being right, should run his own battle. The best captain I have ever had, the best captain I have ever known, challenged the quarterback's judgment, in a firm but kindly manner, not more than six times during the entire season, and on every one of those occasions the captain was right. The quarterback learned to accept these challenges with good grace and profound respect.

The quarterback, and the other players too, should be just as well informed as to the down and distance when opponents are on the offensive. This knowledge materially aids in anticipating the probabilities of play.

The quarter should always be an optimist when he passes the ball to a back. It makes a lot of difference to the latter whether he receives along with the ball a smile which seems to say, "You are good for forty yards on this play," or a scowl apparently implying, "You'll fumble it, for a million dollars." The quarterback's confidence, or lack of it, is infectious as laughter or the smallpox.

On any center buck, or whenever he has opportunity, the quarter should actually deliver the ball to the back, instead of passing to him. Here is an added opportunity to give the runner a fiery send-off, in addition to the encouragement of the voice and eyes. Slam the ball hard against the bucker's body. Instead of retarding his speed it will give him added impetus. The impact of the ball is like a touch of the spur to a spirited horse. The quarter should hold the ball against the back's body as long as he can. The back's onrush will release the quarter's arm in a fraction of a second. Don't be afraid to slam it into him if you can hold it there. He will like it.

Usually the principal correction to make in your quarterback is for lost motion. The handling of the ball, after he has learned to place himself properly, involves no special knack. Any fumbling by him, provided he is cool and the ball dry, is due usually to the center's careless or inaccurate passing.

The quarterback should be placed in a position where he can swing out naturally into a run in the direction of the side he is partially facing. He must be able to get away in the fastest possible manner on the plays that demand especial speed.

The best position for a quarter to assume depends upon the style of offensive formation used. Some of the best teams never play the quarter immediately behind center, but use him as an extra halfback. In this event, of course, his position ceases to be that of a quarterback, for the purposes of this discussion.

With the quarterback close to the center, and the halves and full in the backfield, my conclusion is, after studying various attitudes assumed in this style of play, that he should take the easiest position to make the shortest possible pass to the backs. Therefore, on plays going to the left of center, the quarterback should be close up under the right leg of the snapper-back, in order to make the pass practically a handing of the ball from one to the other. Incidentally, this simplifies the center's work and gives him opportunity as nearly as possible for an immediate charge to carry out his assignments.

The quarterback is now facing, generally speaking, the direction in which the play is going. He avoids fumbles; gets away very quickly; makes a pass short and easy to handle and becomes very valuable in the interference if the play is wide.

Many teams leave the quarterback under center on kick formation. Unquestionably this is done for purposes of deception, an intent adequately proven by the position of the quarter, who is instructed to keep his hands, as on former plays, under center and in a receptive position. This deception generally fails. The quarter, despite instructions, is afraid to keep his hands in precisely the same position he would if he intended to handle the ball. He holds them farther apart and farther away from the ball, lest he fail to withdraw them quickly enough to allow an uninterrupted pass from the center to the kicker. Therefore, it is my opinion that the intended threat of the quarterback under these conditions is mostly lost.

Furthermore, he generally stands with his back toward the side of the line on which he must give protection to the punter. His turn and his charge to oppose his body against a determined assault is often wobbly and ineffective. If the quarterback on kick formation is so placed as to give adequate protection for the punter, no advantage is surrendered. There are innumerable and even increased opportunities for running plays or forward passes. Then why keep the quarterback under center for a deception which seldom deceives?

Once again, the man who is to carry the ball can get away at top starting speed and maintain or increase that speed, because of the simplicity of handling the pass. If the play is to go to the other side of the line, the quarter takes the same relative position, facing toward his right, with his left foot forward and his body close to, and partially under, the left leg of the center.

The immediate objection raised is that these changes of direction give away the side of the line to be attacked, and are therefore of advantage to the defense. It is to be hoped that no coach would be simple enough to give assistance to opponents. He has foreseen that advantage would immediately be taken of the quarter's seeming indiscretion, and the team that attempts to play according to a diagnosis based on the quarter's standing position will find that there are very formidable plays which can be sent to the wrong side. No quarter with a grain of intelligence would fail to take advantage of a team which played a special defense against the side of the line toward which he was pointing.

Wherefore, years of football have shown that against a good quarterback no advantage can be taken simply because a majority of his plays go to the left when he is facing to the left, or to the right when he is facing to the right. And so, without disadvantage to himself, he is aiding the play of the center, handling the easiest pass from center, giving the best account of himself as an interferer and getting the ball to the backs with the least delay and with the simplest, shortest pass.

Right here it might be well to touch upon the question whether the quarter should play the old quarterback position, close to center; or farther behind the line as one of a so-called four-man backfield.

Those who play the latter game successfully cannot understand why the old style should persist. Nor can adherents of the old style understand the preference for a four-man backfield exclusively. Both methods of offense have their strong features.

A majority of the teachers of the old-style position play of quarterback have many strong plays from the so-called kick formation, and similar formations, in which they are really employing the four-man backfield. Their chief objection, however, to the permanent removal of the quarterback from close proximity to the center is based upon the loss of particularly clever work which he can perform in that position. The delayed buck, hidden pass and ever threatening quarterback dive through center are all plays involving the quarter's proximity to the snapper-back.

On the other hand, exponents of the four-man backfield theory claim compensation for the loss of these plays. They maintain that by a double pass in the backfield they can accomplish just as powerful a delayed buck; can use hidden passes of a different sort with a greater power of deception; can hit the center hard enough to gain materially, if insufficient defense is maintained there; and that by selecting a heavier man for their fourth back than is usually picked for quarterback, they can greatly increase their line-hitting power, this extra man being in a better position to lend assistance.

Both contenders are right; but other things being equal I should prefer a combination of the two styles, with a tendency toward the four-man backfield if I were not able to discover an agile, clever quarterback.

Of course, with a four-man backfield, the technical requirements of a center's passing are considerably increased. He no longer hands the ball to the quarterback. He must deliver accurately timed passes not to, but ahead of, the back, so that the ball can be taken on the run. If the play is a center buck, the center must deliver a short, dead pass, which would not carry to the fullback if the latter stayed in his position to receive it. This pass, parenthetically, must be made to an imaginary man about two-thirds of the actual distance from the center to the back who is to carry the ball.

It may be argued that passing into space, or ahead of the runner, is dangerous. In theory, it looks so, but it must be remembered that all good football teams on a run-around end or kick formation do precisely the same thing, if well coached. The pass is not thrown to the runner, for if it were it would be almost a physical impossibility for him to keep up with the fleet interference which started away, or should have started away, simultaneously with the pass.

The greatest dangers in the passing game with a four-man backfield arise from mistakes in signals; the backs starting, or the center passing, in the wrong direction. As a result the long, fast pass sails down the field, with scarcely a possibility of recovery by the erring side.

There is also some danger from miscalculation of the back's speed by the center, when the back is concealing an injury received on the previous play, or is not fully conscious of the severity of that injury or of the degree to which it will affect his starting and running speed.

To adopt the four-man backfield one must have a great deal to compensate for the loss of that coordinating link between backfield and line which under the old style is the quarterback. This dominating personality, standing above and almost upon the line of his opponents, as he gives his words of encouragement and command to his own line and backfield, cannot fail to impress continually upon the adversary an ever-present sense of impending danger. Between teams of equal physical strength and skill, personality is more than half the battle.

CHAPTER XIV: BACKS AND BACKFIELD TACTICS

The traditional fullback was taller, heavier and of knottier muscles than the "light, speedy halves." His function it was to rip up rushlines from tackle to tackle and to endure the abuse of the onrushing blockers. On defense he performed the duties of the modern defensive quarterback, "backing up the line from end to end," in the football jargon of his day. The fullback still persists on the programs and score sheets, but unless he happens to assume the middle position in a parallel backfield and does the kicking, there is nothing to distinguish him from his running mates. The most powerful back of the four usually occupies the position of defensive quarter when the other team has the ball, because of the extra wear and tear involved; but he must be clever in diagnosing plays.

First the face, then niftiness and a powerful running stride, denote the back. Ask yourself first if he looks the part; but give him further trial if he does not, as first impressions are not always conclusive. I like to think of a back who pounds the earth as he runs. The flat-footed runner is the best halfback for a tough grind, if he naturally runs that way and can keep his speed. He is able to change direction, a most vital essential, and he has the legs to drive with.

Let the candidate move about and handle the ball. If he cannot pass it, see if he has aptitude to learn. Watch how he handles it and how he handles himself. Let your backs flit about, scamper about, crash about. Practice them in running down the field, making complete, whirling revolutions in the air, resuming the stride immediately.

Shadow-dodging practice will also give the coach a line on the men who possess fine muscular control. Quick starts will reveal the men who can get away fast. Tackling and blocking at the dummy will indicate men who are likely to develop into sure open-field tacklers. Find the men who have the aptitude and the quick power of diagnosis for defensive quarterback, the job which offers wonderful opportunities for the back with plenty of nerve. In fact, it is the finest one single job in the game.

Having for the time being selected your backs, give them all plenty of practice in punting and in throwing and fielding passes. Use the more promising ones, in fact all of them who show promise, interchangeably, especially during the early part of the season, in the first four or five plays taught, that each back may become thoroughly familiar with the work of every other.

The predicament caused on good football teams by being compelled to shift a back to another position, and this, too, near the end of the season, when the number of backs available has been lessened through injuries or other causes, is altogether too frequent. In fact, it is a useful early season stunt to put the backfield men in the line, so that they may get the knocks that are always the portion of linemen and more fully appreciate their obligation to the line when they return to their regular positions. Also, use line players as backfield men, in order that they, too, may learn the lesson of quick and thorough co-operation between line and backfield, and the hopelessness of gaining ground consistently when the line does not function.

This plan teaches considerable knowledge of the game that can be acquired in no other way, and tends to develop a spirit of willing co-operation that is of tremendous value. There is another element in this arrangement that should not be disdained.

It is the giving to the squad an opportunity to enjoy thoroughly, though in the very best spirit of hard work, the discomfiture and oftentimes ridiculous predicaments caused by these extreme shiftings of players and forces.

The best method of carrying the ball in line attack is described in the course of the chapter on sideline plays and straight bucks. Once a back is running loose in the open, a more individual style is permissible. Many excellent backs carry the ball with one end in each hand, using it as a considerable help in dodging. I have watched this method with careful study. My first inclination was to prohibit it in my own backs, but in every case the player using it had genuine ability, and I generally ended by letting him have his way. Thus far I have had no reason to regret so doing. The moving ball seems even to exercise a mesmeric effect on tacklers. The backs often feint them with the ball as does the boxer with his speedy left. Invariably he back who uses this trick claims that it helps him considerably in his dodging.

Ability straight-arm effectively is a matter of natural gift as well as practice. Very few backs use both arms with equal skill. The others, in order bring the better arm into play, are compelled to change their running direction. The straight arm should not be elected, as a rule, if the back is a fair dodger. The deception of tricky feet is the better reliance, for a tackler with power and determination will smash through the straight-arm, or go under it. Only against half-hearted tackling does it avail, after the tackler has made his final lunge. The proper time for straight-arming is before the tackler has driven in, and it should take him unawares.

The straight-armer dances in on the would-be tackler with a lunge of the body, throwing the legs away while bearing head and shoulders toward the objective, and shooting out the arm in a sudden drive.

While in theory a back running off tackle should carry the ball on the side away from the rushline, I prefer to allow him the use of the arm with which he naturally straight-arms best. After all, there is no certainty as to the side on which he will be called upon to straight-arm.

I do not urge backs to shift the ball from one arm to the other, so as to be free to use a straight-arm. Of course, if a back is being crowded along the sideline, he may have no alternative than to shift the ball and get the free use of his inside arm. But if he has the power of choice, it is usually better for him to dodge.

The arm-split is a powerful upward swing of the arm from a stiff, hanging position, close to the body, to break the partial or half-hearted encirclement of a tackler's arms. It is often highly effective, especially against the forward arm in a tackle from the side.

The same result on being tackled from the side is often accomplished by raising the nearer knee sharply, at the same time twisting the body away from the tackler, with the other foot as axis. This method of escape is often sufficiently effective against half-hearted tackling, or where the tackler is reaching with his arms instead of putting his shoulder to the victim's legs decisively. When you can twist away from a tackler, his body is not in contact with yours.

Dodging is such an instinctive, natural process that it can hardly be described in terms of consciousness. A thousand trifles decide what the ultimate direction shall be; but they all amount to a quick grasp of the weakness in the opponent's body poise.

Uniformity of starting position by the backs is not essential, not even for the moving pictures. It is perhaps advisable to place one hand or both on the ground as a brace, to avoid starting before the ball; but on some very fine teams none of the backs adopt that position. The sprinter's start, while doubtless superior for line-bucking, does not lend itself as well to lateral motion. Therefore backs should be, on the whole, encouraged to start from that position which, after due experiment, seems to be the best position for them.

A back should acquire the frequently useful knack of making an abrupt change of direction immediately before hitting the line of scrimmage. If the play is practically a straight buck he should be equally efficient with either foot. But if his direction is slanting, at or outside the tackle, his more probable and helpful change of course will be in rather than out. In other words, his turn to avoid the tackler should be sudden and toward the inside; that is, toward the center of the line. This sudden turn can be made only by the outside leg and foot. A man can make a slow change of direction by the use of both legs and the bending of his body and head; but an abrupt change only with the foot opposite to the desired direction. Many powerful backs could increase their effectiveness by learning to adjust their steps so that the proper foot will strike the ground at the instant when this change of direction may be advisable.

CHAPTER XV: BACKS IN RUNNING ATTACK

I have heard coaches complain, since the old push and pull game was eliminated, that there is little for the extra backs to do on offense, except in deception. This only proves that these coaches do not understand the principles of co-operation between line and backfield. For if they did they would be very glad to have one or two additional backs on every team. Backs are still of great use in so-called tandem plays, provided of course that they have the necessary punch, to aid a lineman in removing a stubborn defensive player; or, if such aid be not required, to break down the defensive back; remembering that the forward back must not block the hole with his own body, and, if thrown, must try to roll away from the opening.

We call men running ahead of the runner with the ball "interference." Unfortunately the word interference gives too much of the idea of mere protection. It should be the desire and the task of every good defensive tackle and end to impress at all times upon this vanguard of the runner with the ball that they are indeed nothing better than protective. Backs who feel this way rarely advance the runner against a good defense. Theirs should be the spirit of aggression, even more so than that of the runner with the ball.

The runner who expects aid from his fellows, and who seldom pays in kind when the opportunity offers, should not be tolerated. Backs ahead of the man carrying the ball should not specifically protect the runner. He, rather, should use them to protect himself. Their mission should be firmly fixed in their hearts; to rip into and knock down whatever and whoever impedes the advance.

There are two ways of hitting the line: one is to send the back to pick his hole; the other, to compel him to hit the spot the signal called for. It is entirely theoretical whether during a game you make more ground by one method or the other. Oftentimes the hole, though apparently non-existent, is really in the making, and requires only the punch of the runner to swing wide open. The offensive and the defensive lines are carrying on a struggle, one to build the hole, the other to break through and stop the threatened play. They are simply holding their own. Backs should be impressed with the idea that any one of them, with reasonable speed and sufficient determination, can break through under these conditions.

At the start of a game, it is impossible to tell how one line will match the other. Under the first theory of line hitting, the back advances with a waddle, not at full speed, holding the head high and watching for weakness to develop around the spot to be attacked. One of the great university teams of the east pursued this plan, without material success against its chief rivals, for several seasons.

Charging the back point-blank at the spot where the hole is to be made is undoubtedly the sounder theory. Here the offensive lineman is set to a specific task at a specific point. He knows where the back intends to break through; and while he works to open the hole there he has in mind, so far as possible, the intention of not himself blocking the advance. But in the case where the back is sent toward the line with express instructions to pick his hole, there is a strong tendency on the part of the partially successful offensive lineman to cease working, because he knows that the runner may not select that specific spot, and that there may be a better place on the immediate left or right.

Furthermore, in this case a good defensive quarterback has just so much extra time to discover the specific point to be attacked, and to meet the runner head on. And it is questionable whether there is anything that involves so much punishment to the defensive line, or so much weakening effect, as the crash of a hard running back, whether he gains or not.

"Carlisle vs. Dartmouth"
Bain News Service

In the early stages of the game every play that a team attempts may fail to gain its proportion of the ten yards necessary for a first down. This by no means proves that this team will lose the game. The physical changes taking place are, as yet, impossible to ascertain. But the team that is being pounded may be losing more strength than the team with the ball. At any rate, one thing is certain. It takes practically as much physical strength out of a man to run at a line under three-quarters speed to be knocked down as it does to run at full speed and meet the same result. The mental discouragement in the former case is certainly much greater than in the latter. Therefore, while you carry the ball, take as much out of the opponent as possible; and one of the surest methods is by pounding him with a strong attack.

Furthermore, if you work the same play two or at any rate three times against the same team, educated linemen and an experienced backfield will get the true, accurate picture of the opposing lines at the moment the back attempts to break through; provided the linemen at that spot continue a determined effort to open the same hole. The offensive team may not have gained any ground to date; but the linemen should have been taught early in the season that their efforts now will be far from wasted. They have, presumably, taken as much out of their opponents as out of themselves, and have nothing to worry about on this score. They should know now beyond question where the weak spot is, at or near the point of attack, as the two lines struggle to thwart each other. That information should be imparted carefully to the runner; and on the next attempt he should be able, under the very same efforts by his linemen, to side-step at full speed into the point of weakness formerly developed with reasonable assurance of a gain.

CHAPTER XVI: PROTECTION BY THE GUARDS

Countless hours of needless thought and labor have been placed upon the protection of the quarterback by the center and the guards, especially the latter. The old custom of guards and center locking legs still maintains its ancient importance in conservative minds, to such a degree that the makers of the law of football have found it necessary to incorporate in the book, as an exception to the general rule, that guards and center may lock legs. This, no doubt, in order to stem the indignant wave of protest that would follow if this smug little custom of ancient days were forbidden. And so we see the giants of today, like the giants of the olden times, standing with straddled legs. Each guard throws his nearest leg fearlessly and discordantly across the nearest leg of the center, thus making it almost impossible for the poor quarterback to find a place to nestle.

Yet the object of this strained effort is to protect the little general behind. Locking legs is a clumsy arrangement for the center, an unreasonable tangle for the guards and a sore trial for the quarterback. There is some protection, admittedly, but it is a protection given at the expense of ten per cent efficiency in the four men involved. This would indeed be a worth-while arrangement if the center trio were blind, or physically incapable. But at the worst these three men have only to defend the quarterback against two. Their legs are not in a position at all times to do the bidding of their brains.

It must almost be assumed that these three men, if their positions are correct, are not expected to charge, for they cannot do so without unravelling the unfortunate leg tangle. The only other justification for this position is the assumption that the defense is going to get a decisive jump on them. But this is not rational, either, as it is generally admitted that an offensive team will have at least a slight starting advantage over the defense.

No coach would admit that the duty of this trio is not to charge with the snap of the ball. Obviously, therefore, the power of the charge and its direction, principally controlled by the head and shoulders, are the essential elements in effective work. Then why not place them in the most natural and powerful position to do what is expected of them? They are close enough together so that a concerted charge will include the man or men who threaten the quarterback, unless these men assume defensive positions outside the guards; in which case their menace is slight. Furthermore, they then become a problem for the tackles, rather than for the center trio.

If the defensive quarterback emulates the will-o'-the-wisps of football tradition by throwing himself over the rushline to intimidate the passing, a few short forward passes over center will cure him of his ambitions in this direction, ambitions which are hardly likely to be realized in any event.

If your line is going to make a resistance instead of an attack, then spaces should not be allowed; if it is going to make an attack, then spaces are allowable, and, within certain limits, highly advisable. An extra good center and guard could line up safely a foot apart. If they are six inches apart, they will at least have room in which to operate without bumping one another at the wrong moment. I am referring here to a line which knows its assignments and will carry them out with a smash.

The kick formations, however, are an exception to the rule. I am inclined to believe that here the line should be compressed as tightly as convenient to operate. This for the reason that the kick formation, originally entirely defensive, still retains a great deal of its defensive obligation. More and more the theory of defending the kicker is being subordinated to the idea of getting the entire line down under the kick without delay. However, there is still a limited necessity of great importance to prevent the immediate charge of any of the center trio through the line. This is best accomplished by bunching the five forwards from tackle to tackle. These five men, charging with the snap of the ball, will include in their path of advance the center, if he is playing in the line, and both guards. The charging quintet start their charge down the field in the above-mentioned tight formation; strike the defensive trio hard and without fail, and, never really breaking their formation, slip their bodies or hips sufficiently to one side to allow the intending blockers to ooze through, not run through. Immediately thereafter the defensive quintet spreads gradually until its members are in a position to wage war against the receiver of the kick and his helpmates.

By way of interjection, the most serious problem here is not so much to prevent the center trio from blocking the kick as to prevent the tackle-to-tackle quintet from going down the field.

Even with this tight formation on kicks, however, avoid locking of legs by guards and center. The tight formation will give sufficient protection to the kicker against the center trio, provided a high kick is sent away from a point ten yards behind center within two seconds of the making of the pass.

Regarding the proper distance between men on the offensive line in regular formation, the best fundamental theory is to make the line as wide as possible, consistent with safety. The defensive line must balance the offensive line; the defensive guards outside the offensive guards, the defensive tackles outside the offensive tackles. This being true, the wider the offensive line, the greater the spaces between the defensive linemen, and the greater the opportunity for gaining ground. Simmered down, it means simply this: with rare exceptions, such as a very close kick formation, the crowding of the offensive line is neither logical nor effective. Sufficient space to give the individual freedom of action, as well as to widen the attacking line without weakening it, is advisable and should be taught.

The theory that linemen should interlock legs is also based on another outworn convention; namely, that forwards must always face slightly toward center, in order to see the ball and start with it. Both tackles may be men who get their best charge off the left leg; but one of them, nevertheless, must crouch with the left leg advanced, and make his spring from the right foot. One man may be hopelessly placed if he is called upon to swing out of the line in order to get into interference. Yet, regardless of his charge, or his ability to carry out his assignment as an interferer, the coach insists that he stand according to an obsolete rule. The starting signal has rendered it unnecessary for forwards to watch the ball, yet the old tradition persists in arranging the stance of rushline forwards.

There can be no argument that the natural position of the lineman, within the rules, is his best position. But this natural position must be maintained. Except for purposes of deception, a lineman cannot assume a new natural position, so called, after he has heard his signal. Therefore, he must take the position from which he can best perform all his assignments. There is no mystery about these assignments. He has been definitely instructed.

In the case of raw material it is necessary to select for a man early in his career the position that the coach believes to be the best. But as time goes on and experience accumulates, there is nothing to justify a refusal to allow a different position, if results are improved thereby. The words above, "except for purposes of deception," open up a beautiful field for the really clever lineman, the man who knows his plays, who knows the work that he is expected to perform, and who can start from either leg; the man with first-class muscular control.

The best defensive lineman meets his Waterloo in the fellow with the tricky feet.

By changing the position of the feet, together with a slight inclination of the body or head, a nifty forward can often misdirect the defensive man who is looking for early signs that will help him to a diagnosis of the play. I have known several forwards so subtle as to be able to send formidable defenders on wild-goose chases, without the expenditure of any more of their own energy than was required to make some slight but seemingly significant shift of the feet or balance of the body.

The guard must be voracious and patient; voracious when the opportunity presents itself, and patient to wait for it; understanding that while he waits he must expect a considerable amount of disagreeable trouncing. He must be a man who does not especially crave to become a headliner in the papers, but who loves the game for its own sake. He must hope for little credit except from those who thoroughly know football, and while he is contributing his little mite, he must ever expect a reasonably powerful drubbing. His must be the wonderfully cheerful disposition which takes its own reward in the consciousness of duty well done.

It is possible to get along at a pinch with mediocre guards; but in the big game of the season your team can be defeated as readily through mediocrity there as in any other way. The right fielder in baseball may be chosen for his hitting, and sent to the sun-field with a prayer. But history has shown that the prayer is seldom answered. To be sure, if you are reduced to the necessity of using one inferior forward to fill out your team, it is absolutely necessary to play him at guard; but this is only because a lively center on one side and a crack tackle on the other, with a defensive quarter four yards behind, will be able to carry him through a majority of the games. If you wish to see the difference made in a team by the substitution of a first-class, powerful guard for an inferior one, not only in the defensive but in the improvement of the running attack and the aid that a guard can bring to center and tackle, try the experiment, for your own amazement.

In the present game, under many conditions, it is necessary to pull out one of the center trio, to act as a second defensive quarterback. Tackles are seldom picked for this duty, for many reasons. The center-trio man can shift much more quickly and conveniently, and the best man of the three should be picked. If a guard is picked, and the remaining guard is weak, a very dangerous defensive problem may be discovered.

A guard should have a powerful charge, should be able to work fast and successfully on the ground, and must not be a loafer, despite the temptations and comparative opportunities of his position. He must be a glutton for the punishment which he is sure to receive, and which he cannot accept or retaliate, as the tackle may, while occupying any traditional attitude of self-defense. The early Christian martyrs were sinful and worldly compared to the guard who, in spite of the provocations that he often has to endure, maintains an attitude of sweet serenity, and really loves his neighbor just across the neutral zone. "Go thou and do likewise," would be a most unfortunate motto for a guard to follow. Ability to assimilate punishment and to inflict it implies physical strength and a fair amount of weight. The ideal weights for a center-trio playing a low charging defense would be: height, five feet ten to possibly six feet; weight one hundred ninety to two hundred pounds. But, as in the case of centers, many great guards have weighed much less, as others have weighed much more, than the figures indicated. The heavier and taller the man, the more wonderful must be his muscular development to render him efficient.

CHAPTER XVII: ENDS AND END PLAY

The position of end is a tremendous job. More brains, more stamina and more accuracy are required for an end than for a whole backfield. It is the most glorious job in football; a job that calls for the most extraordinary vitality! When you stop to think of an end in a busy game — going down under fourteen punts and twenty-five forward passes, many of them long ones, in addition to his desperate battle with the tackle and all his other duties, some idea is grasped of the severity of end play. No team should be without four good ends, and even then the chances of third and fourth substitutes to "make their letters" are quite as favorable as they are in other positions.

The normal distance of the defensive end from his tackle is eight feet; but the farther back from the scrimmage line that the runner is likely to start, as from a kick formation, the wider of necessity the initial charge of the end, and the greater his distance, therefore, from his tackle. He should stand eleven feet from his tackle on kick formation; the tackle meanwhile having shifted himself some two feet farther from his guard than usual. The end charges for a point where he can meet the opposing backfield bent on skin tackle plays or end runs. He charges direct for that point; the angular charge often practiced being a mere waster of time and energy. Any very slight changes of direction necessary can be made readily and without difficulty during his direct charge.

After all, and whatever the style of line play, the great secret of defense is fast charging ends. They intimidate the halfbacks, make them hesitate, often make them scatter. Forward pass? All right, just try it once with fast charging ends rushing into the backfield, ready to jump for forward passes, or to smash into formations! If the pass can be made, it must be made awfully fast. Moreover, the end who goes tearing into the backfield forces the offensive play to disclose itself immediately. Now, the quicker you can show it up, the quicker you can stop it; especially if it is not a "straight" play, but something else again.

Many of the great university teams retain their ends on the line of scrimmage on plays that seem to presage a forward pass. In the first place, this teaches the end to loaf. In the second place, it gives the attacking team (unless a tackle, or, very occasionally, a center man, breaks through to hurry a pass) the very opportunity that all teams long for. Plenty of opportunity for delay before making the pass is all they ask, whereas a pass that is hurried by the defending team is seldom successful. There are some very quick, short passes to the ends; but these scarcely ever accomplish more than a short gain, and are ever in danger of interception by tall, wide-awake tackles or defensive quarterbacks. The pass that counts is the pass that takes time and calls for accuracy in the thrower.

The place to kill the forward passing game is in the opponents' backfield, and the passer should always be hurried. The end on the offensive should shift frequently. Ends, make a point of acquiring this habit. Especially when a play is going to the other side of the line an end should always slightly change his position, though for no apparent purpose. This frequent shifting gives him opportunity to place himself properly at a time when he needs to give everything he has to dislodge or block the tackle. By this time the latter's suspicions have been lulled by the continual, seemingly meaningless, shifting about of the end.

No end is worthy of the name who neither dares nor is able to work successfully against his generally more powerful tackle opponent. The most positive asset to an offensive team is a first-class end. The region around the defensive tackle offers the best opportunity for ground gaining. The spaces are fully as large as anywhere else, with the additional important factor that the play can be sent there almost as speedily as it can to any other point. It is also very near to the end of the rushline, and therefore more difficult to reinforce. The chances for a long gain are better here than anywhere else. Therefore the end needs all the power that can be given him without sacrifice of the speed he must have for his down-the-field requirements.

"If an End Had Four Eyes..."
National Photo Company

If an end had four eyes they would not be too many. He could use them all. The moment when he decides to rest may be the moment of his undoing. Other players occasionally may have a chance to loaf with impunity, but never the end.

It is lamentable to see the end on some of the biggest and otherwise the best teams, after charging a few yards into the backfield on a kick formation, stop and wait for the run that is already started. He gives the play a chance to form; then backs up with it, using his arms to hold off interferers, showing extraordinary cleverness, oftentimes, in so doing; and physically exhausts himself, only to see the runner continue, with two or three readjusted interferers in front of him. In the old days that was a pardonable sin; for the poor, misguided end had the immediate aid of three defensive backs, playing up very close to the defensive line, one or two of whom were supposed to break interference and to assist the end in picking off the runner.

Today, two of these men, the defensive halfbacks, are so far away that they cannot arrive in time to help the end with the interference. He must strike at its heart as quickly as possible, before it has a chance to form and get under way with real power and speed. On a wide tackle or end run it is not the duty of the end to get the runner. He will get him if he can, but his main duty is to break down the interference. An end goes into a wide tackle or end play with the main purpose of slowing up that play and disorganizing it. If he accomplishes so much, without ever taking an interferer down, he has ruined the play. He has slowed it up at a time when the positive intention of the offensive team has been shown. This subjects the runner and his interferers to the immediate attack of the halfbacks and the tackle on that side of the line; while further defeating the purpose of the team with the ball by compelling the runner to leave his interference.

If the formation made by the interferers and the man carrying the ball is close, that is, if the runner is within two yards of the interference, it becomes the end's plain duty, without hesitation and with all his force, to throw himself across the legs of the man or men who are advancing in the probable path of the man with the ball. The course of the runner extended through to the interferers in front of him is the line of attack where resistance must be applied. The idea is to force a change of direction by the back. The interferers have no means of knowing which new direction the back will elect to take, and cannot, therefore, continue to assist him intelligently. Against a reasonably effective defense there is never time for readjustment. Nothing so discourages a backfield and dashes its hopes so completely as a defensive end rushing through it before it has fairly started.

There are times when the end should not throw himself into the interference, especially when the interference is so far ahead of the runner that there is neither chance to topple him over it, nor seriously to inconvenience him by a change of course. On a run from kick formation, for example, it is seldom that the distance between the pretended kicker and his nearest interferer, as the former begins his run, is not greater than four yards. Sometimes it is six or seven. A charge into the interference would not seriously inconvenience the runner, such being the case. In fact, such a charge, if made immediately, would not be even toward the intended course of the runner. The best end in the world might take down one and possibly two interferers; but there would be several left, and the runner would be neither slowed up nor forced to change his direction in the slightest degree.

On this particular play, the real task of the end is to make a speedy charge to the nearest point along the probable path of the runner at which he can possibly meet him. The end knows the line of advance after the runner has taken two steps, whether it is to be a straight dash outside of tackle until the back meets his line interferers and then takes a wide turn around end; or whether he intends a wide course from the moment of starting. If the latter, the end should charge in so fast that the interferers must actually turn back a little if they intend to take him out of the play. If the end accomplishes this much, namely, forcing the interference back toward the runner, he has practically ruined the end run. The direction of the interferers is now wrong, and probably can never be righted; while the runner is forced to slow down if he intends to keep his protection. Finally, the runner will have to change his course.

If the runner is heading for the outside of tackle, intending to meet the line interferers and swing out behind them, then the end's charge is straight at the man with the ball. Here, again, he must keep his feet, because the distance between the ball and the interferers is too great to accomplish much by spilling them.

The mistake that ends make in this sort of play is to discontinue the forward charge. Every stride of forward charge increases the uncertainty of the runner as to his best ultimate course of forward advance, and also increasingly retards and delays the interference, which, of itself, is almost fatal to the play. The longer the aggressive attack is continued, the longer it takes both interference and runner to get past the danger spot.

The sooner the end stops his advance, the sooner the runner can pick his own path, and the quicker the interferers can reform.

Stimmed up, the end should always leave his feet to dump the interference at the point the runner would pass through if left alone; provided the runner is close enough to the interference to make it unlikely that he will be able to pass anywhere else. If the runner has a chance to make more than one stride, probably he will be able to change his direction. In this case, the end should charge through the interference at the runner; or, if the runner is swinging wide, the end charges to intercept him at the earliest possible instant.

When the end elects to stay on his feet, he should remember that this is the appointed time for a lavish use of the hands.

Ends and tackles both should ever and always charge into the backfield; never behind their own line. Of course, after they discover that a play is positively "gone," they take the shortest possible route to cut it off or to pull it down from behind, but they should not run behind their own line. If an end sees a play aiming apparently at tackle, he charges forward as usual, driving the play inside the tackle, if he knows the ball has gone with the play; but prepared also to stop an end-around-end run or to change his course sharply.

A nervy, intelligent end has no trouble or difficulty with plays that come at or near him; his danger arises from plays that are apparently going away from him. Therefore he should rest never, but always take his charge into the backfield.

Heavy as his defensive duties are, they will not compare with the severity of the requirements made upon him when his team is running with the ball. To make ground over the tackles is impossible without offensive ends who are able to manage tackles or at least hold their own with them. The tackle is heavier, more powerful, and can use his hands. To offset this, the end should have an advantage of position, and he does have the advantage of knowing when the ball will be snapped and the exact point of attack. He probably has greater speed than the tackle, which should be a big factor on the charge, especially if coupled with the greater agility reasonably to be expected of an end.

The end must impress his advantage of position on the tackle by his perpetual shifting; causing him all the worry and mental uneasiness possible in a man of probably superior weight and strength, just as, in the wilds of Africa, the smaller, more tenacious, more active, vigorous and vicious animal has his chance to wear down the larger brute.

The tackle is not justified in following an end out beyond the limit where he can protect the territory inside of him. A pretense of following the end out, for the final purpose of getting an easier entrance into the backfield, is allowable. Defensive linemen must balance the offensive team, and he must shift with the idea of balancing the team, not the individual.

If the end goes so wide as to engage the defensive end, the latter must warn his tackle, and the tackle must warn himself, that a kick or forward pass is in order; or that his own end may be blocked. His duty then is to break up the backfield formation, even if he does not get the runner. The tackle knows instinctively before he has taken one step whether a run is on or not. If it is a run, he has a hustle on his hands. So has the defensive end who, as the ball is snapped, dodges the offensive end if he can, using his hands also to fight his way into the backfield.

The offensive end should play under the tackle as a general proposition; but given superior speed and plenty of stamina, a very fine piece of tactics now and then is to meet the tackle at his own game, so far as the rules will allow. Let the end stand up and take a chance, occasionally. The audacity of the move may have more good effects than bad.

The long, snappy tackle is not having all pie when he is being pestered and knocked to the ground with alarming frequency by attacks directed from the ankle to the knee. It applies to all men on the line that the head and shoulders are the chief implements of warfare, backed up by accurate charge-blocking with the body. The end may not be able to drive the tackle out of the way; but it is extremely difficult for the latter to operate if he finds himself effectually blocked and has nothing left to succeed with except his hands.

It must be assumed that the tackle will often prove too much for the end to control; and in many plays one back is assigned to complete the work which the end has attempted. If necessary, he will come to the aid of the end; but this weakens the play, as it takes away one back who should be of tremendous value against the secondary defense. The end seldom needs aid. It is not that the end individually must show continual superiority to the tackle; but he has advantages enough to make it very difficult for the tackle to work. If the end is able to take up the tackle's attention almost to the exclusion of what is supposed to be the latter's job — breaking up interference and attempting to get the runner — then that end may be said to have accomplished his full duty.

If on the proper side of the man, and having the necessary speed of charge and enough accuracy, it is often extremely advisable and effective so to charge as to meet that leg of the defensive player on which the latter was originally braced. It is the leg which must be first raised for the decisive step forward. Accurately hit while in the air, it means the throwing of the man off his balance. Before attempting this means of attack it is well to know that one is throwing the man away from the play, not into it; though even in the latter case it is sometimes a successful maneuver, because the man is falling out of control.

Slim ends need not be afraid of the big fellow at tackle. One of the coaches of a leading eastern team in 1916 gave me as the only reason one of his linemen was playing on the team that because of his size no quarterback ever ran plays anywhere near him. One good team, by chance or otherwise, later in the season decided to try out this big man, and found him such a wondrous friend to their offense that they continued to hold conferences with him until they had won the game.

Having read over these remarks about the end rush, what a sweet dream to a coach it would be if his end rush might have the weight and strength of muscle of a tackle in addition to his other qualifications!

.

CHAPTER XVIII: THE TACKLE'S BRUTISH CHARGE

The requirements for successful tackle play and the essentials in end rushes are tending toward approximation in modem football. The tackle still requires greater power as between the two; the end a clearer discernment and sounder judgment, combined with better muscular control. It is also very fine to see a tackle who possesses speed, but speed with the end is positively necessary. Both must be fighters, game to the core. For the crux of the situation in football today is the battle between the defensive tackle and the offensive end.

That which used to tell the story of line play is now only a figure of speech. Guard no longer engages guard and tackle the opposite tackle on a man-to-man basis, in a great majority of plays. It can no longer be said that one tackle out plays the other, except as he opens holes better, or plays a more intelligent game. On close formations the defensive lineman plays slightly outside the corresponding player on attack; so that the defensive guard becomes the obstacle in the way of the offensive tackle, while the immediate opponent of the defensive tackle usually is the offensive end.

This is not always true, as there are certain specific plays where the coach will have ordered it otherwise; but it is true of the great majority of plays. As this is so, the natural conclusion of a wise coach is that his ends must be physically capable of putting up a fairly equal fight against a powerful tackle; and this in turn brings us to the statement that a tackle must have power enough to cope with the end.

The tackle, in fact, should be the most powerful and relentless charging forward on the rushline. On the defense, he should charge from the ground, and if the offensive end is playing a normal position, close to his tackle, he must charge through this end, in a direction slightly toward center; he must charge with head and shoulders; with the arms swung sharply from the ground, ready to accentuate and intensify the charge, either to drive the end back, prevent his getting down the field, throw him to either side, or to use him as a fulcrum from which the tackle may throw himself into a play directed outside of him.

It is impossible to impress on tackle candidates too forcibly the necessity of a bold, audacious, crashing charge. If he would be successful at the smallest cost to himself, physically and mentally, the tackle must, by his style and power, convince the offensive end that he, the tackle, is lord of that particular bit of disputed territory and that there shall be no question of the fact during the remainder of the game.

This is one of the glories and great secrets of football; the production of the personality and power, on the part of every single man on the defensive team, to impress early upon opponents a sense of the futility of attempting an advance through a particular territory. Every football player should be taught conclusively that each member of his team when on the defense is prepared to exert every ounce of power and fight that he possesses to drive away the adversary permanently from the place that he is guarding. Any man who is unwilling to guard his own territory in this spirit will find the attack hammering at his door until the end of the day; for he will have been discovered as a weak spot in the line; perhaps as the weak spot in the line.

And the tackle, especially, must have a brutish charge; he must bump opposition out of the way, and he must cover ground.

It is very desirable that his other qualifications be combined with height, because height means reach; and four or five extra inches of reach, backed up by strength, is a matter of great assistance in the struggle with a swarm of interferers. A short, stocky tackle, though doing his best work, often finds himself a bare six inches from the man he wants to reach, and who is brushing by.

It is also almost essential in a tackle that he be able to change his course quickly. But a tackle who can put himself in the enemy's backfield early is accomplishing much to break up formations and cripple the offense. An end and a tackle on either side of the line who insist upon going into the backfield immediately on every play, and are able to accomplish it, leave no alternatives for the attack except center plays, forward passes and precarious punts.

Even when the standing straight-arm defense is used, height and reach are of great advantage to tackles, enabling them to stand off charging opponents at the line of scrimmage until diagnosis of the play is completed.

The tackle, like the guard, must be able to endure a great deal of punishment, but he takes it in a much more romantic fashion and a rather more human position; with a delightful opportunity to fight back and to see the more decisive results of his work.

Until recent years the left tackle was picked especially for his speed, as it was of great importance that he join the two ends in their race down the field under punts. Oftentimes the defense against the ends was so severe that if the punt-catcher was to be nailed in his tracks by anyone, the duty fell to the left tackle. The tendency to put the faster and better tackle on the left very naturally persists; but the reason for it has changed. It is now due to the habit, logical or otherwise, of running a large majority of plays to the right from regular formation; until it would almost seem that most backfield men are right-legged runners, turning on the left leg but driving with the right. Habit and perpetual practice are the only logical excuses for this somewhat one-sided development.

All through the 1890s, the general habit of backs was exactly the opposite. The strongest side of the line on defense was always the right, because invariably the best backs attempted most of their runs against that side.

At any rate, the left tackle continues to be the big noise. When he is graduated, the very excellent right tackle is moved to the other side of center, and the best of the substitutes or newcomers is broken in as the new right tackle.

On offense, the tackle finds the defensive guard very nearly in front of him, and the defensive tackle too far out to handle. The general method of offense, an iron-clad rule that must always be followed, is to get the first man who will interfere with the play. Under nearly all circumstances, therefore, the offensive tackle finds that his battle is to be with the defensive guard. Whether he will receive aid from his own guard depends on the whereabouts of the defensive center. If the defensive center is playing in the vicinity of the offensive guard, the latter must according to one of the first laws of the game take this man out of the way; not only as a general protective measure, but specifically to save the quarterback from serious trouble.

CHAPTER XIX: PLAYS AND HOW TO MAKE THEM

A coach will shift his offense from year to year, although his basic system may remain the same. He adapts his changes to his material, but even if he have a veteran team it is well to make alterations. New plays and formations renew the enthusiasm of blasé seniors, as well as increase the labors of rival scouts, thoroughly familiar with the strategy and tactics hitherto employed.

But whatever changes in his style of attack a coach may find it necessary or advisable to order, the offense that scores is the offense which, whether familiar to the opponents or not, has unanimity of start, fundamentals carefully worked out and a strong punch. There is no great mystery about plays, or the making of plays.

A brother coach or a schoolboy captain writes and asks for a play. You cannot respond intelligently unless you know at least the basic formations which his team is using. There are certain individual, specific plays, good for one try or perhaps for two; but the play your correspondent wants is one that can be put on without changing materially his style of offense. The trouble with most offense is that there are insufficient check plays, any kind of play that has a natural tendency to prevent the defensive players from taking chances by early and immediate reinforcement of what appears to them to be a danger spot.

For example, you have a shift formation to the right, with every indication that the attack will be on that side. A strong check play or two will prevent the defensive team from taking advantage of your shift and charging madly into the threatened area.

Most teams have too many offensive formations, with too few plays from each formation. The plays they use are generally the more obvious ones, with insufficient checks and delayed bucks. It is far better to pick out the weakness of a general offense, so that it can be corrected, than to make a picture book of plays which cannot possibly avail unless the coach knows the little niceties of attack and the general idea of proper assignments. Specific plays explained in this book are of little value unless they fit into the general scheme of offense of the team considering them.

Most coaches should be able without difficulty to devise numberless ground-gaining plays. The chief points to remember are these:

Start at center, wherever the hole is to be built; as you need reasonable protection for your quarterback if he is playing under center. Furthermore, this is the place to start in order to make sure that you have overlooked nothing in developing the hole at the desired spot.

Second, give every man a job. There is more to do than you have men to do with.

Third, never send a man around behind his own line merely to give him an assignment. If he cannot be of material assistance there, shoot him through the opposing line to take down secondary defense; doing which he will incidentally interfere with players of that line who are cutting across to stop plays. Or send him to assist the runner should he succeed in breaking through. This assignment, also, will include interference with hostile linemen who are cutting across.

Fourth, figure out carefully the most convenient man who can be spared from the task of opening the hole and send him against the defensive quarter, who is a tower of strength in your opponents' defense. Sometimes the player so assigned will be a forward, sometimes a backfield man.

Fifth, do not neglect to make the best use of your backfield. Some coaches work plays in which the only backs engaged to bring the attack to the desired point of attack are the quarter to make the pass and a man to carry the ball. They dispose of the two remaining backs without much thought; and this tends to create a certain amount of doubt as to the effectiveness of the play and the efficiency of the coach.

These men may well be used to conceal the attack by making false charges at other points in the line, with the distinct intention, however, of crashing into opposing linemen, both to keep them out of the play and to tire them. Also, the extra backs may be used as fake interferers around the end. To be sure, this hoax is very quickly discernable, but it lays the foundation for a real play from the very same formation, with the quarterback faking the pass and following the other two backs. Do not imagine that you are wasting your backs by sending them on their fake errands. These contradictory moves by backs not directly involved in the attack arouse the deep concern of a first-class football team, and oftentimes very seriously divide the attention of one or more of the best defensive players. Make your backs work all the time. They are strong enough to stand it.

The coach who plots out a play for a team which has a fast start and the necessary punch knows at once, if he knows his opponents' general style of defense, what men must be removed to make the play go. If they cannot be removed, the plays must be avoided, at least for the time being. Many plays are strong against one team and weak against another, according to the caliber of individual players or the defensive methods encountered. The coach must make up his mind what are likely to be the effective plays for a given day, and advise his quarterbacks accordingly. He will not tie the quarterbacks' hands by so doing, although he may, for a sufficient reason, the secret of which he need not necessarily share, advise against, or even prohibit, the use of some particular play. In general, his advice to the quarterbacks as to the plays they ought to use constitutes a tip, based on his knowledge of opponents.

The one last touch that gives permanent distinction to a well drilled football team of all-round strength is its possession of an outstanding star player, a giant among strong men. But I would rather have a fine team of well distributed ability than a star surrounded by mediocrities. If the coach does have the dangerous and fascinating custody of a genuine star, the temptation to build an entire system of offense around him becomes almost irresistible. Certainly he should frame his plays to give the star man his best chance. But the coach ought not to sacrifice sound football, as injuries or the faculty may cause the star to set. By using the star player as a threat, ordinary plays can be given additional effectiveness, his own part in them being merely deceptive. But unless these plays are serviceable enough for everyday wear and tear, they cannot be relied upon if for any reason the star is lost to the team. Do not put all your eggs in one basket.

CHAPTER XX: THE ESSENCE OF OFFENSE

One hallucination that many coaches and quarterbacks labor under is that in order to break the spirit of the opposing team it is well to hurl plays against the strongest man in the line; which plays, if successful, will accomplish the desired purpose. Focusing plays on the star lineman is sound policy occasionally as an experiment, or when the opposing team is breaking up and you aspire to its complete destruction; one man being seldom able to stop plays alone consistently. Under such circumstances, running down and ramming over the star lineman usually completes the rout of the opposition. But it is the extreme of absurdity to start an offense on the principle of attacking the greatest strength when both teams are fresh and neither has obtained an advantage.

There is a double risk in such a course of procedure. Not only will failure add to the assurance of the team attacked, but the same failure will give rise to serious doubts among the members of your own team as to their ability to gain. Furthermore, why is it not better on general principles to play through any man in the line rather than the strength?

Everything favors attack on the weakest man as the logical idea. A chain is no stronger than its weakest link. Even this must not be overdone. Success at the weakest point will draw help from the player on either side, which will make the going more difficult. Whereupon the quarterback should direct his plays on either side of the original weak spot. When the defending players in consequence revert to their normal positions, then attack the weak member again.

If the center is a rover it generally means that the two guards are playing a bit closer together than if he were in the line, for there is always the threat of a dash by the quarterback through center. Inasmuch as the tackles cannot draw in any closer whether the center is a rover or not, the width of territory to be defended between guards and tackles is therefore increased. Disregarding the defensive play of the center, there are the weak spots in the line. But on straight attack we may not disregard the defensive play of the center, as he is in a particularly strong position. If, however, he can be drawn to the wrong side, for example to the left side when the play is to go to the right, there is developed an extraordinary opportunity for a substantial gain. This leads to the conclusion that a delayed cross-buck, under good cover, should be a gainer. Or a feint at center, with the ball carried just outside of either guard, would, by drawing the center back into his normal position, uncover the weakness between guard and tackle.

Plays against tackle are the foundation of any scheme of offense. It must be so. Any confusion on the part of the defending team, any inefficiency by the tackle or end, opens up a beautiful opportunity. Deficiency at the guards is offset in great measure by the work of the center and tackles, backed up by the defensive quarter; but even occasional and momentary weakness at the tackles may be fatal.

The essence of the offense is to get the jump on the defensive line. This cannot be disputed as a general proposition. It would be useless to take this advantage without following it up. There is bound to be, against a strong team, an immediate defensive shock as the two lines meet. But with the advantage of the getaway there should be greater power in the offensive line at the first contact. If the attacking line merely gets the jump and expends it in the shock, stopping there, no real advantage has been gained.

The lesson is, drive while the driving is good. The legs should be brought up fast and hard, in short, jerky, powerful strides; the head set firmly in line with the spine, the muscles of the back, shoulders and neck distended. It is when one leg is raised in a long, slow effort to place it forward and continue the drive that the weakness in its owner develops, and he is hurled back or to either side by the faster-stepping, more powerful opponent. In a drive, the faster the feet hit the ground, the surer the hole.

"Runner on the Field"
Harris & Ewing

Do not take a man out, or order it done, to the right or to the left. It is hard enough to take him out at all. All college coaches have been asked, from a hundred to a thousand times, whether the particular lineman inquiring shall take his adversary in or out. I have always answered: Never mind the direction. Take him. Get him out of the way. And, knowing where the play is going, after you get him at a disadvantage, slap him into the most harmless place.

An offensive lineman at first is in great difficulty against a standing defensive player who holds him off with his hands. This defensive player acquires the habit, after he has used the method for a short time, regardless of his specific instructions, of jumping into a powerful brace immediately after the snap of the ball, instead of a possible charge; the result is that if the play comes at him he has no time to develop a charge, and must fight it out on the scrimmage line.

If the attack is powerful, this means, at the best, stopping the play after a slight gain only. In jumping into this brace he acquires the habit, as soon as he learns the heights of his opponent's shoulders, of shooting out both hands and arms in their most natural pose, that is, evenly. By this I mean each hand an equal distance from the ground. The offensive forward can easily develop a charge with one shoulder down. This will result in the defensive man losing one shoulder, thus throwing himself sufficiently off balance to be removed easily by his opponent.

There is another method if the offensive lineman has time; which he has on delayed bucks, intended to pierce the line at or very close to his position. This is, to make a fake charge with the shoulders, following it up immediately by the real charge. It leaves the defensive lineman stripped of his defensive power. His arms have been jammed forward and have met nothing. His poise for effective work is gone. The rest of him probably will go with his opponent's head and shoulders.

Mix him up, get him so confused that he will lose confidence in his arms and in his defensive instructions generally, and you will soon find him down on the ground, where he belongs, but where he does not know how to work. The standing defense players stand up with equanimity in the center of the field; but most of them are found on their hands on the ground, trying to stem the tide when there is danger of being scored upon. I would much prefer to stop my opponent in the middle of the field than be compelled to do it on the ten-yard line; not so far as the thrill, but so far as the outcome of the game is concerned.

There are innumerable offensive and defensive positions that a man can be thrown into by the action of his opponent, even when the latter is being outplayed. If the play is continually stopped, however, the defensive lineman is satisfied with his defense. This is where the offensive lineman has his opportunity to put the play up to the defensive quarterback at least. He knows, at every moment throughout the play, just where the spot is, though shifting slightly from time to time, almost big or weak enough for the charging back to break through; and by a slight shift of his body at the instant when he knows the back is to strike, he can increase that opening.

Right here lies the golden opportunity. Strange as it may sound, the offensive lineman and the offensive back should have sufficiently retentive memories to store away this knowledge for future use; and surely the back should receive this information, if he does not acquire it himself, from the lineman or possibly from another back who discovers it.

So it comes down to this: in the early moments of the contest the teams are figuratively sparring for an opening. Neither may be able to accomplish much with its attack. But the team that discovers the holes a foot or two removed from the spot where the coach intended or expected them to be, will soon make the formerly impregnable line take on a decidedly different appearance.

Eyes were made for football. Do not forget your eyes, whether in the so called "blind" charge of the defensive line, as it charges with stiff neck but with forehead sufficiently turned up to enable the vision to take in all that is happening, or whether in the back as he peers into a hole or selects the correct moment for the straight arm or the arm split.

Some of the best defensive players are what might be termed "football gossips." They have eyes and ears in the backs of their heads. They are out for information at the expense of their opponents at all times, as they should be. Coaches and players should religiously guard against giving to the opponents one iota of advance information. Watch the backs in practice every minute, and do not allow them to discover to their opponents by so much as a glance, shifting of the feet, or inclination of the body, the translation of the quarterback's signals. It is amazing how much some defensive players can help themselves by reading aright the trivial signs and signals that denote intention and which should never be given except by an occasional clever back who gives them only to mislead.

Overdoing this deception is much to be avoided, but a back or a lineman can occasionally open a beautiful hole without physical exertion by a deceptive glance, a movement of the body or feet or a carefully worked out over-balancing of the body. And here, while we are on the subject, it is well to state that the lineman who, upon hearing the signal for a play that calls for him to open a hole, immediately responds by a shudder, a more resolute pose and a crashing of his heels into the ground, would make a better man to receive the drubbing in practice on the second team.

CHAPTER XXI: RUSHLINE PLAY IN LINE ATTACK

Let us take the working-out of a play where the ball is to be carried between the defensive left guard and left tackle. In the first place, the entire problem starts at the center of the line. Therefore, the first question is, whether the defensive line consists of six or seven men. If six, there is an extra defensive quarterback. Logically, then, one of these two at least must be taken care of. And if the system of attack with a seven-man line includes the problem of reaching the one defensive quarterback, the system with a six-man line includes the problem of reaching both defensive quarterbacks.

The seven-man defense is the better defense for most regular formation plays, and hence will be considered first. The defensive center becomes the first serious consideration, since he is playing in the line.

If the center is on his own right of the offensive center, the latter must be able to make the pass and to cut off or charge back this opponent. Now suppose that the clever defensive center, who, as the signal started, had purposely drifted out to his own right, now makes a sudden, slight shift, which places him on the other side of the snapper-back's head.

The passer's obligation alters immediately. He is no longer in a position where he can hope to guarantee the safety of his quarterback. And the offensive right guard who had other plans before the opponent shifted to his side of the center, is unable to take the chance that his own snapper-back will be able to protect the quarter under the new conditions. The positive duty of driving the opposing center away from the quarterback and keeping him out of the play now devolves upon the guard.

Had the defensive center maintained his original position on the other side of the snapper-back, the duty of the offensive right guard would then be determined by the position of the defensive guard. If the defensive guard were playing wide, the offensive guard would have the evident duty, and the delightful task, of shooting through the line and attempting to take down the defensive quarter. If successful, he would increase the chances of a gain very materially. If his speed and skill were plainly insufficient to accomplish this purpose, he must help as best he could against the defensive center, in case of any possible danger from the latter, or against the defensive guard, continuing the work which by this time the defensive tackle would have begun; for beyond question, under the rule stated with reference to the guard, the tackle must put all his strength upon the defensive guard if the latter is in his natural position, between the offensive tackle and guard.

Having charged the guard with all his might, and finding that for reasons sufficient to his own guard the latter has elected to help him; and having, temporarily at least, cut off the defensive guard from advancing to the point of attack, the tackle now slips off his opponent, and attempts to throw himself into the path of the defensive quarterback.

The chance that he takes by leaving the defensive guard for his own guard to handle is well worth while. By this time, he knows that, so far as his work is concerned, the most likely man to stop the play is now the quarterback, rather than the guard. Furthermore, the man with the ball is now about to reach the scrimmage line; and as between the two, the defensive guard who has been temporarily held up, and is now engaged with another man who should finish the job; and a fast-charging defensive quarterback, who thus far has met with no opposition, the guard becomes of minor importance.

"Not So Bad"
Frank A. Nankivell in "Puck"

This double task by the tackle of dealing with both the guard and the defensive quarter often can be done, and often has been done. It is most beautiful and effective work.

If for any reason the tackle finds the defensive guard playing in so close that he will be easily managed by the offensive guard, his problem then becomes this: "Who is the next most likely enemy to prevent our advance?" Beyond question the answer is: "The defensive tackle," if the latter cannot be handled by the end. And here the decision must be made. It is better to gain a yard than a shorter distance; and if the defensive tackle is in a position to get to the play faster than can the defensive quarter, it is plainly our tackle's duty to aid his end. If, however, the end is showing entire ability to keep the tackle out of the play, the defensive quarter becomes the offensive tackle's objective.

What of the remaining forwards? They cannot be used behind the line of scrimmage on a play of this kind. Their work, therefore, lies ahead of them.

If the left guard is speedy enough to block off the defensive quarterback, it is plainly his duty to do so.

Here let me warn against a very common practice which, despite unnecessary, hard work, accomplishes little in comparison with the physical exhaustion entailed, and should therefore be avoided. Many teams are coached on plays of this kind to charge their opponents who are in front or outside of them, in order to prevent their sliding along behind the line and aiding in the defense. But the true task of the left guard, if unable to reach the quarterback, is to swing over in front of the point of attack and head the runner, with the idea of blocking the first opponent who arrives on the scene.

The left tackle, likewise, should attempt, if possible, to cut across between the defensive guard and the point of attack, with the idea, also, of heading the play and blocking. In any case he must get through the line as fast as he can. Should he find that the defensive guard opposite had aided in preventing or stopping the advance, he should make special efforts, on the next similar play, to prevent this guard from repeating.

The left end should charge slightly to the inside of the spot where the defensive right tackle stood when the ball was snapped; thereby automatically and effectively preventing that defensive player from sliding across to the point of attack in time to aid in the defense. There is great importance in discovering early in the game the particular players who are preventing advances, and laying special emphasis on preventing them from doing so in the future.

Now the great point to be brought out here is that the guard and tackle on this side of the line should be blocked off in their effort to defend on the other side by the offensive charge as it breaks through to head the play; rather than by a specific charge against individuals. In the former case, the offensive forwards can accomplish both a proper disposition of their opponents in the line and help to the runner. In the latter case, further effectiveness is impossible after the direct blocking of the opponent.

This completes the offensive theory of a play aimed between defensive left guard and tackle, except for the work of the backfield, purposely omitted because I wished to point out carefully the assignments of the forwards, regardless of the backfield attack formation, provided the attack is a direct thrust by any of the backs, on a regular formation play through this point.

The action if the attack were finally put through this point by a delayed buck would differ according to the amount of deception, and the amount of defense that was drawn away from the point of attack by the deception. Of course, the only defensive men of particular importance who are thus drawn away are the men who can return upon discovery of the deception. Those men are easy to pick out. They are the men who probably would withdraw the least from the actual point of attack, and the men, fewer in number, who, if left alone, might be drawn toward the point of attack. The former should be allowed a moment in which to move with the deception before being charged; the latter should be charged immediately if they are dangerous.

It is of infinitely greater importance to work out the theories of attack and defense carefully than to offer several diagrammed plays, which can never be put on properly unless the instructor knows the basic theory. On the other hand, if the theory is perfectly understood, it is the simplest matter to make innumerable plays; many more, in fact, than a coach should use during a season.

To demonstrate further these ideas, let us take the same play against a six-man defensive line, with two defensive quarterbacks, one of the latter being a center-trio man, drawn back about four yards to assume a position behind and between the defensive guard and tackle; the regular defensive quarter moving over to a similar position on the other side of the line.

There are two things that become apparent at once. First, the defensive line being of exactly the same width as before, the spaces between the men on the line are greater. Second, if we spent so much time attempting to block off the defensive quarter when he was alone, it is especially important when there are two such men, to give attention to the same idea. There is a third important consideration which should be mentioned here: a quarterback in the old-fashioned but still sterling position, close up under center, becomes a greater menace than ever; with the apparent result that the defensive guards are forced to a position somewhat closer to each other than if they had the help of a center in the line or only slightly withdrawn from it (the "roving center").

Starting once more at center, the point of attack being still between the defensive left guard and tackle, there is, in this case, no defensive man, provided the line is even, in front of the snapper-back. Without question, then, this center should be able to pass the ball and by his charge to cut off the defensive quarterback on his left.

But if that is his assignment, nothing else appearing, his quarterback is seriously exposed to the defensive right guard. This fact immediately establishes the work of the offensive left guard, who must at once charge across and cut off the dangerous man opposite to him. These two things accomplished, what about the right guard on offensive? If the defensive guard opposite or slightly outside of him is not charged immediately, the menace to the quarterback once more becomes especially serious. For example, suppose an offensive right guard attempts at once to charge against the defensive quarter, already presumably cared for by the center. If for some reason, right or wrong, the right tackle has charged elsewhere than into the defensive left guard, the latter, charging, and finding no opposition, crashes accurately and destructively into the quarterback; and the play is ended with a material loss.

Thus the lesson is taught again most forcibly that the offensive lineman must always attack the first man who can injure or stop the play.

The moral is: always get the first dangerous man. Therefore, this right guard, having a guard almost opposite to him but slightly on the outside, must defend his quarterback by driving his man out of the way and preventing his return. If he can manage this defensive guard absolutely he notifies his own right tackle of this fact; but, even then, the right tackle must note carefully how far over the defensive guard can get before the offensive guard loses his power to control him. It is a matter of inches only. Therefore, in spite of the apparent ability of the offensive guard to control the defensive guard, if any doubt arises in the tackle's mind, because of the slightly changed position of the defensive guard toward the tackle, the latter also must charge the guard. This charge will be only momentary. He will leave one guard to the other as soon as he can, and attempt to reach the second defensive quarterback, really the main dependence now of his team. The surer the offensive guard of his ability to control the defensive guard, the more positive becomes the chance of a big gain, because the tackle is then left practically free to put the nearer defensive quarter out of action.

But this immediately raises the question again, will not the defensive tackle stop the play? The action of the offensive end will answer this question. He has at least an advantage in position. This is especially true if the defensive tackle is standing high.

Furthermore, the defensive tackle is never so uneasy as when the offensive end is standing outside of him. Here is a play where the end especially desires to stand inside the tackle, and gains a clear advantage by so doing. In fact, he should be able to prevent the tackle from stopping the play.

Meanwhile the offensive left tackle, the defensive guard having withdrawn slightly toward center, can hope no longer to cut through on the inside. He charges, therefore, by the most direct path to cut off the nearer defensive quarterback; failing in which, he assumes the regular play of an interferer.

The left end's assignment is the same as it was against the seven-men-on-the-line formation. Incidentally, it is always vastly better judgment, where the blocker and the man to be blocked are separated by a considerable distance, to rush to the vicinity of the man carrying the ball and do the blocking there, rather than attempt it further away. The man who is finally to be blocked is bending every effort to get at the runner with the ball. The nearer he draws to the runner the smaller opportunity he has to avoid being blocked without foregoing his purpose, and the easier it is for the blocker to find him.

CHAPTER XXII: SIDELINE PLAYS AND STRAIGHT BUCKS

Some of the worst errors committed in football are due to the failure of the coach to drill his team in the plays necessary and the best method of getting away from the sideline. Of course, there is always the well known method of running the ball out of bounds, thereby securing the privilege of carrying it in as far as fifteen yards. But suppose a case where the offensive team finds itself close to the sideline, with only room for the guard outside of center, perhaps not even that, on a third down. Plainly now the ball must be gotten away in one down, if the fourth down is to be saved for a punt or try at goal, forward pass or other scoring play.

The tackle and end of both teams, having no room to play between the ball and sideline, must go to the other side of center. Surely this is handicap enough against the team carrying the ball, as its probable direction of attack, barring a sideline play, is known. The defensive men who have gone over find it perfectly natural to take their places on the unaccustomed side of the line and to tear into the backfield. The offensive tackle and end, however, have no means of knowing what positions these men will take; nor, without coaching, have they satisfactory knowledge as to just what to do.

What they should do depends entirely upon the intention of the play. For example, suppose the extra defensive tackle and end assume positions in the vicinity of the other end, leaving a wide space between him and the regular tackle. If the play is one which starts wide for the end, cutting inside him finally, it would be foolish for the extra offensive tackle and end to move out to give battle to their former opponents at the extremity of the line. Plainly they should take positions immediately outside their regular offensive end, ready to charge on the secondary defense; or one of them to help the regular end with the tackle.

"Sideline Play"
Harris & Ewing

As a general proposition, the principle of offense in the line must always be fight the first loose man who could get to the play. This idea should be taught carefully, to prevent mental confusion arising among forwards when they encounter novel defensive methods. Such instruction further prevents the forwards from wasting their efforts on men already taken care of.

In passing let me say, that the sideline play will never be old.

The old-fashioned end run, except when a four-man backfield is employed, is passing into the discard. As a matter of fact, on regular formation, attempting anything on the offensive farther out than a skin-tackle play is a questionable effort. Plays at or around the end by deception, such as kick formations or double and triple passes, are possible and advisable. But from close formation, with a balanced line, or an unbalanced line for that matter, except possibly on the short side, where the defensive end is closer, it takes too long to get the backfield to the line of scrimmage.

Moreover, during the process of getting to the line of scrimmage, the backs are running for the most part with the sides of their bodies toward the defense. Their merely lateral resistance is subjected to the direct power of the defenders. Their efforts are further weakened by a fast charging end, who if he is successful disrupts or scatters the interference.

Players, however, should never be allowed to consider their wide -running plays as merely intended to relocate the ball on the field of play, if such plays are given and taught to them.

One of the best plays to get the ball away from the sideline, in order to be able to take advantage of a diagonal wind in kicking, or to avoid the danger of punting out of bounds, is a quarterback run based on the deception of a straight halfback buck through guard and tackle. So far as I am concerned, this and similar plays are much to be preferred to the ordinary end run. To make the run effective, however, the defensive team should have been taught to expect the line attack, and it is well to have at least one old-fashioned end run for possible use in getting out from the sidelines in the early moments of the game.

For the straight buck, the backs are in straight, parallel formation, four and a half yards from the line of scrimmage and a yard apart. The ball is passed by the quarterback, in this case, to the right half, who will charge between defensive guard and tackle. Most coaches are afraid of this play, on account of the danger of a fumble. As a matter of fact, there is no excuse for a fumble. The quarterback, however, needs considerable practice.

The chief thing that he must guard against is lost motion. Having placed his hands under center to receive the ball he should not, as is a common fault with quarterbacks, draw the ball in toward the stomach. From the point of receiving the ball to the point where the pass is made one continuous, slightly curved motion suffices to send the ball in the proper direction.

The pass on straight bucks is not made to the back, as this would mean that he must receive it on the side; thus slowing up his speed, which is the chief element for success. It is a short pass, made into the air, at the height of the runner's waist and in front of him. The back's right elbow is held near his side, with the forearm and open hand extended at right angles to the upper arm and fingers spread wide. This hand is used merely to stop the ball. The left hand is held three or four inches below the right, open, parallel to the ground, palm upward, and not far enough from the body to leave a space through which the ball might drop when stopped by the right hand. The ball should drop into the left hand.

If the pass is a bit farther forward than the halfback expected, the right hand must be extended to stop it. In this case the left hand goes with the right, in the same relative position as before. What happens to the football is this: the right hand stops the ball, which, while dropping into the left hand, is encircled by the right hand and wrist, and the two hands together draw it firmly to the chest.

Never forget the motion of drawing the ball to the chest. It helps the runner to bend forward and strike hard with head and shoulders, his protective muscles in the very best position. When the motion of drawing the ball to the chest is completed, the left hand and wrist, like the right, encircle it. The impression given is that of a man folding his arms. The ball is almost completely covered by the forearms, wrists and hands.

Incidentally, this is the best method of carrying on all quick thrusts and bucks through the line, where the straight arm is of little or no avail, but where both arms are absolutely necessary to insure the safety of the ball. This position of carrying the ball and hitting the line gives a back the greatest assurance imaginable. I have never seen it used except by my own teams, but I consider it not only a strong guarantee against loss of the ball, but the method which concentrates the maximum of muscular power. There is here no tendency to carry the ball under one arm, even supported by the other hand, a position in which, on account of the unnatural strain on one side of the body, the straight-ahead hitting power is impaired. The ball, when carried as I have suggested, is hugged to the middle of the chest. The method is natural, quick, easy and efficient.

Should the back succeed in breaking into the open sufficiently to consider the use of the straight-arm, he has a sure grip on the ball with both arms and can quickly and securely transfer it at his option.

Returning now to the straight buck, let me say that this is one. of the fastest plays in football. It cannot be stopped without gain by bringing aid to the line. If the runner is stopped without gain it must be done by the defensive guard or tackle. The defensive quarterback is the main reliance of the defense, but he can-not arrive early enough to prevent a substantial gain. Naturally, therefore, the three men in order of importance considered by the offense are the tackle, guard and defensive quarter. It is one of the few plays which, when properly executed by the quarterback and halfback, can take advantage of the small hole that is bound to be opened for an instant by a fast-charging tackle and end, but may be closed very abruptly. But the defensive guard or tackle must block up the hole conclusively in order to stop a gain. This is a difficult task against a capable end who is charging the tackle and a tackle who should have the defensive guard at his mercy, on account of their relative position in this particular play.

The offensive end, who has the more difficult problem, should find out very early in the game whether the tackle will go out with him when he shifts, wide, and how far. If he can succeed in drawing the tackle out even a foot, although a yard is much better, he should acquaint the quarterback with this fact immediately, suggesting this particular play. Having thus deceived the tackle into the belief that he is endeavoring to place himself for a skin-tackle play (in which case he would prevent the tackle from coming out), he is now in a position to shift his charge quickly and cut the tackle off.

Assuming that the defensive guard and tackle are effectively blocked, the next man to be considered is the defensive quarterback. A fast right guard should be able to reach this defender, as he has no one to interfere with his charge. He need not defend the quarterback, as the pass is so rapid, unless the defensive center is a man of extraordinary speed. Even in this case, if the snapperback, immediately upon the release of the ball, throws his body toward the right guard position, that protection undoubtedly will suffice. The left guard, left tackle and left end charge through the spaces to aid the halfback if he succeeds in clearing the line.

Now we come to the part of the play wherein many coaches fail. It is evident that the other two backs, originally parallel to the runner, cannot contribute directly to his success. But these backs must be given a task that will have a specific, helpful, practical result. They must not be wasted. In cases of this sort, many coaches dismiss the extra backs with too little thought, giving them, perhaps, a fake retreat into the backfield as if to receive and throw a forward; or sending them crisscrossing without sound reason.

On this particular play, note the natural result of the assignment of the two remaining backs. Their duty is to start immediately with the snap of the ball for the defensive left end; not one behind the other, Indian file; but the fullback outside the left half, so that each has a chance at the end.

There is one very important thing to be said here which applies especially to backs. Every man who is sent on a deception assignment, unless especially instructed otherwise, must be a good actor. He must be realistic to the last fine shade. If he is not, the mental picture drawn for the benefit of the defense is insincere, and the latter will not and does not react as hoped for by the maker of the play. And so, in this case, if the two backs do not dash out at top speed and take a bump at the end they will have done serious injury to their offensive.

Suppose the charge by these two backs is especially realistic. Note the results. First, on the defensive tackle. The picture his mind receives of the play as it starts is blurred. He has a vision of a possible play inside of him, another of a possible play outside of him. During his uncertainty as to his best plan of defense, the end buts him. The defensive quarterback receives the same inconclusive impression. He, too, has his fractional second of extra uncertainty as to the point where his services will be required. The defensive end finds it expedient to give most of his attention to avoiding the two backs, but he, too, is perplexed.

All of these things not only materially assist the runner with the ball, but also contribute to a beautiful setting for another play, which is not only a fine ground-gainer, but to which I have already referred as one of the best for getting the ball away from the sideline, in order to improve the kicking or running situation. This play contains the same assignments as the actual buck in nearly every particular. The quarterback receives the ball, and makes a natural feint, as if to pass to the halfback; who appears to receive it, slaps his arms, double over and crashes between defensive guard and tackle. The defensive quarter, having seen the original play, with the halfback carrying the ball, has his mind temporarily but firmly set on stopping that halfback without gain. This is fine for the attacking team, for the halfback is instructed that the defensive quarterback will be coming for him and in a perfect position to be cut off from the wide run that is planned.

The defensive tackle, having seen the original line buck also, has only one purpose: to nail the line bucker in his tracks. Accordingly, he falls victim easily to the offensive end. If, by any chance, the defensive tackle snaps into the hole so quickly as to elude the offensive end, the latter continues his charge and nails down the defensive quarter.

The attacking quarterback, on previous line-bucks, has avoided giving any suggestion to the defense of the possibility that he may or might run with the ball; and now his fake pass, to be thoroughly realistic, involves a very slight element of delay. He may need better protection than when he merely passed the ball. His right guard, there being now other and better means of reaching the defensive quarter, accordingly devotes himself to blocking the defensive center, thus affording the necessary protection to his quarterback. But if the defensive center is on the further side of the offensive center, the guard will, as before, charge for the defensive quarter. If he misses him, he can at least continue on to the wide wing, to give his aid, with the forwards on his left, to the runner with the ball.

Meanwhile the quarterback shoots with the ball under his outside arm for the territory outside the defensive left end, passing immediately behind the supposed line-bucker as the latter enters the line.

Now we come to the defensive left end, who is being sorely tried. He has acquired the habit of avoiding as well as possible the two wild backs, who are continually hurling themselves upon him whenever the straight buck is played. He is mentally and physically in the worst state possible to stop a play which he does not expect. If he does expect the play, to stop it will be difficult, with no aid from the tackle and probably none from the defensive quarterback.

At least one of the backs attacking the end should stay on his feet, and both should do so if they are sure, by the position of the end, that by merely blocking him the runner will be safe. They can then continue on their course with the very important task of taking down the defensive halfback on that side, who has discovered the nature of the play and is on his way to rectify the harm done.

I have seen this play gain over two hundred yards during one game against a good team. Its full value is obtained by withholding it until the opponents have defended against the actual buck two or three times. Needless to say, the success of the end run depends upon two things principally; on how well or poorly the straight buck operated, and the efficiency of the two halfbacks in deception when the quarterback is not coming behind them with the ball.

CHAPTER XXIII: SEQUENCE PLAYS IN THEORY AND REALITY

What the pitcher in baseball accomplishes by change of pace, a football general sometimes attempts by means of a series of plays prearranged in order and carefully rehearsed, thus suddenly increasing the speed of the attack, since no time is lost in giving signals between plays. A sequence is supposed to rattle off as fast as the attack can line up. The speed of it ought, theoretically, to sweep the opponents from their feet, especially where the element of complete surprise is present.

The modem football match is geared to a slower gait than the parent games of the nineteenth century and early twentieth. Quarterbacks cannot run their teams with the speed and abandon shown in the old days of five yards to gain. They have, nowadays, to consider and choose among a greater variety of more complex plays; including plays designed for particular situations, which depend for success upon particular positions assumed by defenders, and especially the secondary. Hence series plays ought to contrast sharply with ordinary speed of attack. Inject a sudden sequence into a deliberate and slow advance, and, if successful, it catches the opposing team faster than it can Ime up. Unless the defenders recover instantly from their consternation and readjust themselves to the change of pace, the going is often easy.

Sequence plays are wonderful, except for one thing: no sooner do you get them started than you find out something on account of which you would prefer to stop them. They are very apt to disorganize most teams using them. There is seldom a concerted plunge on the part of the whole team. Penalties for offside are frequently deserved. Worst of all, a string of plays run off in sequence wakes up the players of the other team; and it is often far better to let them sleep. A sequence is such an exciting thing that it enthuses everybody.

There are so many intricacies, so many unexpected things arising during the course of a sequence that it is very often better to stop it after one or two plays. Moreover, a sequence is quite likely to result in a heavy gamble on the fourth down, with two yards to gain and a punt the logical alternative to another running play.

In addition to the difficulty on sequence plays of getting one's own men back on side quickly and properly braced for the snap of the ball, there is usually the ultra-clever defensive player to be considered. This individual manages to tie himself up, innocently of course, with an offensive player's arms and legs, preventing all attempt at a speedy lineup and also giving his rattled mates a chance to steady down.

It is further the weakness of this method of attack that some one defensive line player, roused to the danger, and making a fine defensive plunge against a forward who is not quite ready, is able often to set the poor old sequence back several yards. This special spurt will raise immediately the gravest question as to the advisability of continuing the sequence.

There is much debate generally as to whether three plays or four should be included in a sequence. Personally I believe that a two-play sequence is the best, to be started on a first down; leaving two downs for readjustment in case of failure. But my experience has been that a good team against which even a two-play sequence has been attempted becomes at once the liveliest and most wide-awake aggregation imaginable. It becomes, in fact, deplorably and disgustingly alert.

Generally, sequences are run off on the snap of the ball, no signal numbers being given after the first play. Sometimes a -snap signal only is given after the first play. The team is less likely to start off like a bunch of stragglers if the snap signal is used. Even with a snap signal in use, the ragged offense of the attacking team often overbalances the strong points of sequence plays. It requires a vast amount of drill to accustom players to line up fast after the first play of a sequence, ready to start again with the snap of the ball. When these series plays were new and novel they were highly successful in many instances, but it becomes increasingly difficult to upset a well coached team by their use. I question whether a sequence of more than two plays is worth the amount of time that must be put upon it to get results.

CHAPTER XXIV: LONG AND SHORT FORWARD PASSES

———————————

As a rule, forward passes from a set formation are much less effective than those thrown unexpectedly from a running formation, with the defensive backs already on their way to protect the spot threatened by the supposed run. Under the latter condition, coaches and players can figure to a nicety the probable position of the secondary defense at the time the pass is to be thrown. This greatly lessens the chance of interception, even when the thrower's accuracy is only moderate.

The one general law regarding forward passes is to throw them when possible ahead of the runner as he is facing. He is surer of the ball and surer of an additional gain if he can field the ball while in motion. However, the pass, if particularly quick, must be thrown accurately to the receiver. Short forward passes can be thrown equally well by any man in the backfield, if five yards behind the line, assuming equal proficiency among the backs; but many of the very effective long passes are thrown to best advantage by the quarterback behind the deception of a fake running attack. Other deceptions such as double or triple passing may be employed to give the eligible receivers time to get down the field. Or the long passing may depend for execution upon the original deep backfield position of the thrower, as in a kick formation. Placement kick formations provide a particularly effective mask for forward passing intention.

The forward pass may be said to have accomplished its original mission in football. That was to keep the defense sufficiently open and sufficiently in a state of uncertainty to render it possible to make ground consistently by running attack. Even when the pass is only used as a threat, its primary purpose appears to have been achieved. In fact, it may be questioned whether the rule-makers have not gone a little farther than they really intended. They have given the offense a weapon with which, when expertly used, no defense can cope. Almost any coach can devise forward pass plays against which there is literally no protection which will not weaken beyond hope the scrimmage defense of the team attacked. Fortunately, the human equation enters in to save the situation.

The forward pass is a great disorganizer of a team which is excellent against straight attack. This team is often tight against the strongest plays at or around the tackles; but let two successful forward passes be thrown, or even one, and the effect on scrimmage defense is often surprising. Unless the pass is restricted, offense will incline, I think, to its use more and more. There are many possibilities in the way of forward passes completed behind the line of scrimmage which have not been realized. As a team could gain consistently were it not for the defensive quarter, evidently forward passes directed behind his position will continue to have at least a fifty-fifty chance of success, and against long passes there is really no adequate defense that will not hopelessly weaken the defense against running attack.

It is a mistake to grip the ball in making long forward passes. In bringing the ball sharply around in the act of throwing there is sufficient resistance to give control and to impart the necessary spiral twist, provided the three longer fingers are firm on the part of the lacing nearest to the end of the ball, which is balanced on the palm and thumb. But while drawing the ball back behind the ear, where it is held pointing toward the right and rear (in the case of a right-handed thrower), the left hand is used to press it firmly against the right hand, and this pressure is relinquished only in the act of throwing. The ball is really thrown sideways, but as the thrower's arm completes the arc which points the projectile in the direction intended, he twangs the lacing as he snaps his wrist, thus imparting a definite rotary motion to the ball.

Long passes should never be made to the runner, but into a zone beyond and preferably inside of the runner in the general direction of his flight when the ball is thrown. When he changes direction to field the ball he will be able to see it by a slight turn of the head without loss of speed.

He may also discover any special danger of interception.

Some of the best long forward passes I have used start apparently as cross-tackle bucks, with the quarter under center.

The backs give every appearance of making a genuine line play. They charge the end and tackle, while their tackle takes the guard. The quarter, having faked his pass to one of the backs, hustles to a point five yards behind the tackle, taking advantage of the backfield's protection. He makes his spiral pass to either end, although the more diagonal pass is the easier to recover.

The ends have gone down the field in a wide course, in order to run past and around the defensive halfbacks. The latter are forced to make their turn inside of the ends, who when twenty yards down the field are some fifteen yards outside of the half-backs' original positions. These backs are never able to field a pass of sufficient carrying power, or even to overtake the runner, provided the latter is not compelled to wait for the ball; the ends being fairly on top of them by the time the ball is in the air. The end is going at full speed, and with perfect assurance, to a zone known to him and unknown to his opponent.

A pass carrying twenty-five yards beyond the line of scrimmage cannot be fielded, in fact, by either the halfback or the fullback. This statement might be incorrect in case the fullback makes an immediate guess as to which of the ends will receive the ball. If he backs the wrong guess, a touchdown results. If the ball is thrown poorly, too near to the center of the field, the full back may recover it; or he might have a fair chance to field the ball if he were playing closer to the line of scrimmage than he ought; in which event the quarterback would no doubt have elected the surprise kick instead of the forward pass. As the ends are at least fifteen and often twenty yards down the field before the fullback can be certain of the direction of the ball, and as they are in motion while the fullback is not, the latter's chances to interfere with passes up to forty yards in length have practically the value of a zero from which even the cipher has been eliminated.

The receiver can watch the ball and the halfback while running, while the halfback must lose sight of the receiver if he turns to look for the ball. So that the advantage remains with the attack, even if the pass is a trifle short. Of course, if the pass is altogether too short, the halfback may be expected to get it. There might be such a thing as a pass too short even for the halfback. But the problem of getting distance is generally the least of the passer's worries. The ball has only to be thrown with sufficient height to "stay up." The great difficulty is to find ends who will run and not lag, and who will field the ball as an outfielder in baseball fields the drive over his head.

Covering the last fifteen yards with arms outstretched has cost many a receiver many a pass.

His first duty should be to get under the ball. The best ends let the ball come to them, have a neat basket of hand, chest and forearms ready for its reception, and continue the run without losing a stride. They have timed their speed to effect a perfect junction with the arrival of the ball.

Another very dangerous pass is thrown behind the deception of a center buck, on which it depends, in fact, as the defensive quarter must be drawn into the line. The tandem forming on the left, the quarter fakes his pass while swinging around to his left foot. He must remember to point his left toe sharply at a right angle to the scrimmage line, as his next move is to take a long step with his right foot, another with his left and another with his right, which swings him into position for his throw. The pass is taken six to ten yards over center by either of the ends, one long, one short. The ends time the pass, and the one certain of his ability to make connections hails the other with the familiar "I've got it," or "I have it," of baseball. The other end, relieved of his responsibility for the pass, turns his attention instantly to the nearer defensive halfback, and prepares the way for a run.

Preliminary to both of these pass plays the ends show every intention of nailing the defensive tackles, as usual, but as the latter, no less than the defensive quarter, have every reason to expect a line play, they will, if necessary, throw the ends down the field, rather than attempt to impede their getaway. There are many other passes, and they all place a tremendous burden upon the secondary defense. It must know the combination of both defenses, against running plays and against passing. If passes are used continually, the defense will set itself for them; but too often the tendency will be to play the halfbacks too far back or the fullback too far up.

CHAPTER XXV: THE ONLY
STARTING SIGNAL

All teams on attack should use a starting signal, rather than attempt to watch for and charge with the snap of the ball. Few teams, however, have possessed a starting signal which gave them a clean-cut edge on the defenders, as such a signal should do. Starting signals generally in use afford the teams using them such a slight and problematical advantage over elevens which cling to the ancient method of keeping all eyes on the ball, charging on the snap, that there is little to choose between the two methods, so far as the starting is concerned. There is, however, a slight recommendation for the commonly used starting signal in that no player except the quarterback has any cause to watch the snap of the ball. The men on the line, and perhaps one back, who are so placed as to have great difficulty in seeing the snap of the ball without turning their heads, or bending their bodies slightly out of the best charging position, are relieved of this necessity.

Signals should be as simple as possible; easy to acquire and memorize; easy to change in case of detection, without causing confusion, because the fundamental principle remains substantially the same. It then becomes supremely important to possess a starting signal which effectively conceals the moment of starting from the opponents; which enables a team to disregard watching the ball; which enables it to charge with, not after, the snap; which eliminates all nervous tension due to waiting, in strained and listening attention, for a number to be uttered or repeated, one knows not when; which no uproar of cheering or blare of band music can drown; which permits of perfect preparation for, and resulting unity in, the charge.

The string of numerals barked out by a quarterback as the teams line up contains a play number, variously arrived at. It may contain a so-called key number, telling when to listen for the play number. Sometimes, as in the more primitive methods of signal giving, the players are numbered, and the signal contains a number representing the player who is to take the ball. In this case, the spaces between the men on the line are also numbered, and the number of the space selected as the point of attack must also be included in the signal. Finally, we have the starting number which when heard or heard repeated sets ball and team in motion and begins the scrimmage.

Usually the starting signal in question is a certain number to be given and later repeated; the snap of the ball following immediately on the repetition. Sometimes the snap is made on the number following the starting signal, or the starting signal repeated.

Sometimes the signal is merely permissive; the center snapping the ball as soon as he chooses after, but not until, the significant number is given. Sometimes the starting signal is the repetition of the play number. Another method is to snap the ball on some predetermined number in the signal sequence, the fourth or the fifth or the sixth. Sometimes it is the key number which is repeated to give the starting signal.

None of these methods ever accomplished the primary purpose of the starting signal, which is to produce absolute unity of attack, simultaneous with the snapping of the ball; an advantage over the players on defense, who are always compelled to watch for the actual movement of the ball, or the start of the fastest opponent, in timing their own charge.

Take, for instance, the start on a certain number in the sequence following the play number, on the fourth number, let us say. Assume the play number to be 36, following a key number the second digit of which is 9. The complete signal is as follows: 42 — 27 — 89 — 36 — 3 — 6 — 8 — 5. These four numbers are snapped off in regular, accurate cadence, and every man on the offensive team charges on the exact instant when the number 5 (the fourth number) is being pronounced. There is a perfect unity of charge and not the slightest loss of time after the snap. Charge and snap are simultaneous. But the continual charging on the fourth numbers after the signal number becomes so obvious that the defensive team cannot fail to pick up the idea very early, with the result that a defensive charge ensues which is just as well timed, and much of the advantage is lost.

Or let us take the method which involves repetition of the second digit of the play number as the snap number. Assuming the play number as before to be 36, the same signal would run: 42 — 27 — 89 — 36 — 51 — 23 — 46. As 36 is the play number, the whole team is watching for the next 6, in the second digit of some number yet unknown. When the number finally does come in the form of 46, it is just about as big a surprise to the offensive as to the defensive team. There is an unnecessary, nervous tension, because of the uncertainty of the team with the ball as to when this number is to be announced. Result — not a charge as a unit, but a charge as soon thereafter as each man can accomplish it. The former method has half the idea of the correct starting signal, but gives too much information to the opponents. The latter method fails.

The old method of watching the ball and starting with it means a delayed start, and in certain formations one or more players are almost unable to see the ball as held in position by the snapper-back. There is absolutely no advantage in clinging to this method of starting with the ball.

Here is the only starting signal method which combines everything that can give entire superiority to a start on the snap of the ball. Let some number, as the one before or after the play number, contain the starting signal. It may be the first digit of a double number. It may be the second. It may be the result of adding the two, or of subtracting one from the other. Then, grasp the meaning of this starting signal. It does not mean a start on the repetition of the number when heard. It does not mean a start after as many additional numbers have been given as the signal number indicates. It does not mean a definite preparation like that of a sprinter who awaits the explosion of the cartridge in the starter's pistol. It means that the quarterback shall call off his numbers in rhythmic staccato; and that every player knows how many numbers he will have to wait. He makes his charge with, not after, the utterance of the starting number; the charge, the snap and the quarterback's bark all going together.

Now for example, let us say that the addition of the first two numbers makes up the play signal; in this addition, the second number should never be larger than five. I have seen many players who were poor on signals but have never seen one who could not add up to five. This addition becomes so instinctive that at the end of one week it can scarcely be called addition at all. Thus: $26 - 5; 27 - 4; 28 - 3; 29 - 2$ become 31 when uttered, and without mental effort. The next number of the signal is what would be termed the starting signal. It is not literally the starting signal; in fact it seldom is. It signifies on which number, of a series of single digit numbers to follow, the ball will be snapped.

Take an example. The play is to be number 31, the starting signal so called is 4. The quarterback calls out: $28 - 3 - 4$. Then comes an appreciable break, the length of which depends upon the period of the season. For the first week or two the break is sufficiently long to make sure that everybody has the very easy signal. Sometimes in the early season I have had the quarterback repeat the signal, without request from the players. The three numbers are known to include the entire signal. The team is set. The break after the signal, 28 — 3 — 4, having been completed, every man on the team now knows that his play is 31, and that on the fourth signal number called by the quarter the ball will be snapped and the team will be off.

Now the quarterback announces in even rhythm, not varying his spaces between numbers one iota, after the habit is acquired, 3 — 7 — 9 — 8—4 — 6 as many numbers as he pleases. On the number 8, the ball and team go. There is no waiting to find out what the number will be. It may be any number from 1 to 10. But everyone knows it's the fourth number. The number, the snap of the ball and the charge of the team are simultaneous. The team merely says: "I'll count with the quarterback, one two, three, go!" The center says: "I'll count with the quarterback, one, two three, snap!" The quarterback says: "They are counting with me. Let's all count together," and he simply calls out, "Three, seven, nine, eight," instead of: "One, two, three, go!"

The numbers following 8, which is the fourth number, are merely a cloak, and are oftentimes, in the enthusiasm of a hard-fought contest, never uttered. I would advise that the quarterback call out at least one of these meaningless numbers, in order not to give too great emphasis to the fourth (in this case).

In order to make sure that the lesson is understood, let us give one further example. We will say that the play number is 36. Signal: 31 — 5 — 3; then the break, equivalent perhaps to three or two seconds according to the time of the season; then the quarter continues: 9 — 6 — 4 — 8. The ball is snapped on 4. The quarter knows it, the entire team knows it. At the very instant that "4" is uttered, the entire movement, including the snap, occurs. Neither center nor line nor backs wait for the number. There is no offside, no starting before the ball.

The center must pass the ball, if at all, at that precise moment. If there is interference with the snap, or if for any other reason he decides not to pass it then, he does not pass it at all. The line and backfield may charge, because the center has had no opportunity to notify them of his dilemma by calling out, "Signal;" but there is no penalty attached, for there has been no movement of the ball, and therefore no play.

"Gee, But You Look Funny!"
Will Crawford in "Puck"

I give this in its very simplest form, for demonstration. There are numberless combinations to accomplish the same thing. For example, you may make the first number of the signal the key to the starting number, as I prefer to call it. Or you may make the addition of the digits of the first number, or the third number, or any number, the key to the starting number. For example, 21 — 27 — 4. In this case the two digits of 21 added make 3. On the third count in the complete signal following 21 — 27 — 4, each of the three numbers being pronounced on absolutely even rhythm, the entire team takes its plunge. In this case it will be seen that, as before, we are adding the signal number, 27 and 4. The play is 31. For example, let us make the key to the starting signal the first number, and for purposes of explanation let it be one of two digits. We shall add the two digits to obtain the key to the starting signal. Let the number be 21. To avoid any confusion we shall add the second and third numbers to obtain the play signal. We shall call those two numbers 27 — 4. This means that the play is 31, and we are to start on the third number which follows after the break, as before. The completed signal will now be, 21 — 27 — 4; 8 — 6 — 4 — 9. Remember the break after the completed signal, 21 — 27 — 4, in order to give the team opportunity to digest the complete meaning of the signal. The snap and the charge and the number "4" are simultaneous.

After many years' experience with this starting signal, I can scarcely recall an instance when my team was penalized for offside or starting before the ball. Teams have been penalized for standing offside, or where some back, after a quick shift, became overbalanced, and was in motion when the snap signal was given. But these instances were in no way attributable to the starting signal. With all due regard to modesty, I am convinced that this is the best starting signal ever used.

There is no straining of ears, no mental anxiety lest the repetition of a certain number be missed. Nobody is off his balance or unready or unsteady when the count is completed. It is a one-two-three-go proposition, with absolute periodicity of rhythmic count, impossible to miscalculate or to miss. Even if the noise from the sidelines is so great that the players cannot distinguish the numbers that are being called and can only hear the voice of the quarterback, that is sufficient.

Certain numbers are preferable to others for starting, because of the punch that is in them. The more encouragement and fight the quarter can convey by his command to charge, the better the response. Four is the best number of all, 1, 2, 8 and 10 second best, 3, 5, 6, 7, and 9 least desirable. This information is really for the quarterback. The men will go on any number. Repetition of 4 or of any of the numbers from 1 to 10 can do no appreciable harm, because the team is starting while the number is being pronounced.

Simple arithmetical processes, so easy that they scarcely call for mental effort, are to be preferred every time to the waiting for a key number which win be followed by the play number. Nervousness and anxiety are to be avoided rather than a childishly simple problem in addition or subtraction. Never add or subtract a larger number than five. This gives you five combinations for your signal. Numbers ending in a cipher, where addition or subtraction is used, should be avoided. Players are sometimes uncertain whether the quarterback has said 30 — 4 or 34. Elimination of key numbers gives one less cause for tension and worry.

I have used the same system of signals for years. For the first two weeks of the playing season add your first two numbers for your playing signal, and use your third number as the key to your starting signal. Then shift to the very same system, except for the substitution of subtraction for addition; never subtracting a higher number than five, just as in the addition never adding a higher number than five. After two or three weeks at subtraction, with the very simple alternative of going back to addition, in case opponents appear to be detecting the signals, I shift to a third very easy method. I use double digits for the first three numbers, and take the second digits of the first and second numbers for the play number, and the second digit of the third number for the starting signal. Let us say, for example, that the play signal is 28, and the starting signal is the fifth number after the break. Here is the complete signal: 32 — 48 — 25; 4 — 6 — 9 — 8 — 3 — 7. The second digit of the first two numbers make 28, the break comes after 25, and the charge comes simultaneously with the pronouncement of the number 3.

I have used three sets of signals similar to these for many years, and have yet to find any serious difficulty in making the change from one to another.

I shall merely mention that I have found it advisable to have the odd numbered plays nm to one side and even numbered plays to the other. As this is a very common custom, and as simple as any, I doubt if it needs any further comment. However, by way of double assurance, it may be well to say that if my center buck to the left of center were 31, the same play to the right of center would be 32.

Coaches and players often wonder why their signals appear to be known to the opposing team, especially in the second half. They are convinced that their signals were carefully covered, and were known to themselves only. Yet here is the bald fact staring them in the face, and to their own great disadvantage. The mystery becomes clarified when we consider that nine out of ten coaches have one punt signal only; and that formulated according to the same system as all their other signals.

Stealing signals is not considered decent by any coach who would hope to retain his self-respect, nevertheless one meets a coach now and then who will condescend to this method of winning a game, or attempting to do so. He is not in any sense analogous to the player who during a game, and by perfectly legitimate means, through the frequent repetition, for instance, of a poorly disguised signal, is able to anticipate a play and warn his teammates. The unscrupulous coach places a man on or close to the sideline, who writes down four or five or six punt signals during the first half, also the signals given for some particular running play, generally a powerful one, and one frequently used; a skin-tackle play, for example. The punt signal, under the above conditions, is the key to the entire signal system. The spy has these four, five, or six signals, each unquestionably different from the others, but each carrying signs of similarity sufficiently plain to show by comparison the general scheme. The possessor of these ill-gotten gains rushes out to his secret comer, and in a comparatively short time, having verified his discovery of the punt signal by finding the same formula correct as to the tackle play signal, is able to produce to his master the complete story.

A careful coach must guard against this possibility. In order to do so he must have several punt signals. This gives the dire plotter a very different and difficult problem, for when he finds that adding or subtracting numbers, or first and second digits, or any other calculation, leads him to an evidently erroneous result, he may and probably will be unable to solve the puzzle in time to make the solution of any benefit.

In the very large colleges and universities, where material is plentiful, it may be advisable to subdivide the entire squad into Squad A and Squad B. In a general sense the team for the year will be picked from Squad A, barring an extraordinary development by some player in Squad B, which demands that he be transferred. Squad B will be composed of ineligibles, transfers, men restricted by other faculty regulations, and timber for future years not considered good enough or necessary for the present season.

Under these conditions an entirely different system of signals for the two squads would be considered necessary and advisable. It can be seen easily that a team from Squad B playing against Squad A, with a different system of signals and starting, can furnish a much more satisfactory workout, especially from the standpoint of the varsity's defense. But in the general run of football teams, even some of the best, there is no such enviable embarrassment of riches; they are fortunate if they are able to bolster up their varsity team with first-class substitutes, when not compelled to scrimmage one side of the line against the other in practice workouts. In their case, it would be wholly futile to attempt to have one set of signals for the first team and another for the second. Such a course would compel the first team substitutes to learn two sets of signals. The less mental burden of this sort the better for the player.

It is far from satisfactory that each team must know the other's signals. It gives to the varsity team on defense a greater advantage than it deserves, against its weaker opponent; makes a genuine try out and full development impossible and weakens the instinct for diagnosing plays.

In order to offset these unfortunate conditions as much as possible, one of the coaches or extra players can be placed behind the defensive quarterback of the varsity team, to give the second team its signals by holding up the fingers. If the play is thirty-eight, he will call out "Signal," then hold up three fingers, followed by eight fingers. The quarterback then rattles off a string of numbers, meaningless except as it does contain a starting signal. This process may be continued throughout the afternoon with the waste of very little time, as the coach can himself, or through his assistant, order always and promptly the plays on which he desires to lay especial emphasis.

An ultra-modem complication is the giving of "defensive signals." The team not in possession of the ball which indulges in this practice is ever loud in its declaration of innocence, always maintaining that the man selected to give these signals has been especially coached to detect plays, has shown a miraculous power of diagnosis, and has no intention to annoy or upset the attacking team. The rule regarding unsportsmanlike conduct, and its provided penalty, should be sufficient to protect the team in possession of the ball against this particular form of petty persecution.

CHAPTER XXVI: ESSENTIALS IN SCOUTING

Scouting of opponents has become a thoroughly established custom, despite the expressed displeasure of a number of those who consider it an abominable practice. These visitations are considered a proof of good sense in football circles, and I find it difficult to sympathize with those who hold that it is unsportsmanlike to take advantage of anything that a prospective opponent may reveal in his public exhibitions, especially where admission fees are charged. It might, however, be argued, with a good show of reason, that spectators at practice ought to regard themselves as friends, or at least as neutrals, toward the team whose guests they are. This view of the matter, if generally accepted, would, it seems to me, solve the problem to the satisfaction of nearly every one. Incidentally it would do away with the abuse of excessive secret practice, which tends to weaken a close, enthusiastic relationship between the football team and the school or college body.

The distinction between scouting a team in practice and in games is sufficiently a matter of commonsense and common understanding. The stranger appearing on the field at practice who gives ground for being regarded as a probable spy is not infrequently treated almost as a spy would be in war; whereas it is a common custom to notify the coach of the team that is to be scouted in a game of the intended visit. Usually the notification is accompanied by a request for a few of the best seats. Under these frank and friendly conditions, for which all coaches can vouch, it is difficult to see wherein the critics of the custom of scouting have serious grounds for adverse criticism. At any rate, all coaches are aware that their team will be scouted. They know, too, that the scout will begin his task by focusing his attention upon the center-rush, as the logical starting point of everything.

"One Side, Please!"
Herbert Johnson for Associated Newspapers

The chief thing to know about the "enemy" center rush is whether he has different styles, actually used in a game, of passing the ball. It would seem hardly likely, at this late day in football, that a center should have one method of making his short passes and another, decidedly different, for his punt passes. Yet I have found this to be the case on many of the biggest teams.

It can be seen at once what a tremendous advantage is given to a rival team by advance possession of this knowledge. For example, if the opposing quarterback calls for a kick formation and remains under center, but the latter, by the position of his hands on the ball, shows the defense that he intends to pass to his mate in the punter's position, the possibility of line attack can be excluded immediately. The value is entirely subtracted from a formation otherwise not without its good points; for did the center refrain from giving the play away, the quarter could keep the defending team in doubt up to the last possible fraction of a second as to whether he would take the ball either to run with it himself or to pass it to another for the same purpose, or whether the ball would be passed to the kicker for a punt, run or forward pass. But if the center by some fault or mannerism reveals his intentions, the word can be passed along immediately by signal to ends, tackles and secondary defense, who need no longer worry as to line attack, and may adjust themselves at once for an end nm, forward pass or punt.

One of the best potential teams I ever saw spoiled its season by having two methods of passing from center, the one for long, the other for short passes. No doubt, football strategy as it grows subtler will often manifest itself by pretended irregularities in passing; and centers will become versatile in such deception. A center instructed to camouflage his intentions by mixing up his passing, now and then using his long pass technique in delivering the ball to the quarterback, might be able to accomplish the undoing of the cleverest defense. But after watching the center's passing for the eleven to which I have referred, the scouts, after several games, discovering no intent to deceive, were able to put that team at a decided disadvantage in its most important games.

Once informed as to the habits of the "enemy" center with regard to passing, a coach would proceed to ask his scout whether the rival team played a zone offensive and whether a four-man backfield or with the quarter under center. Next, as to the defensive plan; with special regard to the exact positions of the men in the secondary defense; how far the ends station themselves from the tackles and whether the ends charge in fast or play a waiting defense; whether the center defends as a rover, whether the line employs a stand-up, straight-arm defense, or charges from a position on the ground. Next in point of significance would be considered the habits of the quarterback, the position he takes on formations, and his favorite plays.

Some quarterbacks develop a habit almost approaching a dis-ease of taking the ball themselves for a dash through center when the distance to be gained is less than three yards. The coach is interested in any information revealing this tendency, or concerning tricks or mannerisms by which the quarterback is inclined to reveal any of his intentions at any time. The coach's eagerness for indications that plays are apt to be "telegraphed ahead" applies also to the backs and to all other members of the team scouted.

Some quarterbacks cannot refrain from directing their signals or their eyes at the halfback destined to carry the ball. Often a quarterback shifts his whole modus operandi, with even a per-ceptible alteration in the tones of his voice as he gives the signals, when he finds that he has picked himself to run with the ball. Frequently, in addition to giving the signals, he begins talking. Usually, in this case, his remarks are intended to enable him to get away, as in case of a dash by himself through the center of the line, while his backs are standing up.

When a team is working on a starting signal, carefully hidden, the quarterback frequently becomes nervous over one feature, namely that the center pass the ball in time to enable him to handle it. He is quite likely to throw his hands open, or make some other gesture to which the center responds. If the defend-ers in the center of the line discover this failing, they can charge, very often, before the offensive backfield starts, thus more than balancing the usual handicap of the defense, which seldom has that advantage. The scout would be questioned closely as to the punting. He would be asked whether the punters inspected were forward passers also, or dangerous runners with the ball from kick formations. The coach would inquire how many men were called upon for punting, whether any lineman was drawn back to perform this duty, and which was the best kicker amongst them. Did any of these men seem to place his punts.? Did they stand close and kick from running formation, or, if they stood back, how far from the center? How did the centers pass from kicks? On the regular starting signal, or when ready himself, or at some signal by the punter, as for example a sudden opening of the hands? Was there any specialization in blocking kicks; and, in the protection of its own kicker, where in the line was weakness revealed?

To all of these questions, the coach who is keen must require answers in detail; and the scout should be able to indicate within a foot of ground the relative positions of secondary defense players and ends on kicks and regular formations.

Are they charging from the ground on the defense, or standing the attacking forwards off with their hands? If charging from the ground, whether the charge is carried through with determination? Or, if the standing, straight-arm defense is used, do the defenders show an immediate, well defined effort to back up plays on the other side of center?

These are the vital things in one-game scouting. There are many other things for the scout to watch and report, if he has time and opportunity, and the coach naturally will ask many questions not here enumerated; and of course going into the passing game with the scout as well as possible. The coach should also inquire as to any special defensive formations, for example the defense against a spread line, if exhibited.

It is a great aid to a coach to have at least one first-class scout, more if possible, who can watch future opponents in their preliminary games, and report accurately on the significant features of their play. The scout must have a thorough knowledge of the game, combined with genuine reportorial ability; and if he is also a coach, who can assist in "putting on" the rival teams' formations with the second eleven, so much the better. It is advisable for a coach, if he intends to make coaching his business, to judge a scout cold-bloodedly by the results of his work. It is easy enough for a would-be scout to tell an interesting story. The serious question is: was his observation accurate and his information helpful?

If the game is of sufficient importance, the coach should himself see the opponent play at least once, even though he have entire confidence in his scout. There is nothing like seeing with one's own eyes and in actual competition the team that one must defeat if possible. The experience gives added confidence to the coach and to his own team, which argues that he saw the adversaries in a game, and therefore the information he is giving is reliable.

Whether the players, also, or any of them, should be given opportunity to see their principal opponents in action, is a question which cannot be answered by yes or no. As a general proposition, it is better answered in the negative, inasmuch as a positive affirmative must so often be withheld.

The advantages, whether for effect on your own team, or on opponents when they learn that their rivals have seen them play, are wholly psychological. So are the disadvantages. Circumstances alter cases.

There are many men who, though fairly competent in their own particular assignments, are yet unable to confine themselves to these phases while watching the play of an exciting game. They at once become merely spectators, and the progress of the ball commands their entire interest. They emerge from the spectacle with a confused and unreasonable sense of their future adversary's strength or weakness, which depends entirely upon whether said adversary has won or lost. Palpably, such men should be kept at home, at their own knitting, until the day of the great game arrives.

But if you have two or three good men, who command the confidence of your team, and who can be spared from the home game, by all means take them along to see the big adversary play. One of the number should be your best quarterback, who should sit with you and to whom, from time to time, you can point out a significant thing.

If, as is done by some colleges, the chief rival is watched in every game it plays, and also, whenever possible, while at practice, both scout and coach should make out lists of things to be watched. As the season advances, additions can be made to this list. Ordinarily, however, the rival team is observed in three games, at most, and often in only one. If a team is observed only once, the scout will have all he can do to portray the general outlines of what he sees. There are, even then, many details on which he can be prepared to report. And if he can show the formations that rivals use, and their general style of play, his coach will know at least what to expect on regular attack.

It is unnecessary for the scout to attempt to watch and diagram every play. Instead let him diagram plays of particular strength, or unique characteristics. There are a few general questions which a coach would naturally ask a scout returning from a "foreign" field with his budget of information, but in getting down to details the discussion naturally begins with the work of the center of the rival team. The center is the logical starting point of everything. It is the beginning of the game, and may be the finish of the game if the snapper-back is not a thoroughly competent man. A false move by the center knocks the foundations from under the whole attack.

CHAPTER XXVII: PUNTING ---
THE SURPRISE KICK

───────────────

For punting, the quick kick is the quintessence of effective kicking. It is far and away the favorite of coaches who value the element of complete surprise. This punt from a regular formation never fails to amaze and confuse the defending team, even before the result of it can possibly be known. It may be a well placed kick that finds the defensive fullback too close to the line and sails over his head. It may be a kick that finds the same player advantageously placed to recover it, with no special disadvantage to him or to his team. Yet the seed of uncertainty has been planted in often fruitful soil: the sensation of being up against a dangerous opponent. This kick, no matter how often tried, never fails of its disintegrating effect upon opponents. I am not sure that it is not as good a kick as any, even on fourth down, when properly employed by a cool and clever team.

The team that is known as a dangerous forward passing aggregation, especially with long passes, usually can count on a tendency by the defensive fullback to creep up on the rushline. A deep defensive, played by a speedy runner, would be much better, as a charge in the wrong direction from a position too close to the line is often fatal. The defender cannot tell positively until the ball is in the air what its direction is to be. Nevertheless, the defensive fullback often seems to be drawn forward as the moth by the flame, until suddenly the ball is booted over his head on a regular formation play, filling with consternation the defending team as they see their hapless fullback pursuing the bounding leather, his chances of returning it reduced to nil and the chances of a fumble increasing with every stride.

There is no kick like the quick kick for ruining the nervous system of the defensive fullback and his mates. Often it spoils them for the remainder of the game. This surprise kick makes the defense grow old fast. It makes opponents give you credit for more stuff than you ever had. Combined with a little extra bit of luck, it often gives the team employing it a tremendous and decisive advantage.

The kick is easy to accomplish. It makes little difference which of the backs kicks the ball, so far as the formation is concerned, provided the kicker is in a natural position to receive a direct pass from center.

He should be placed in the formation at least three yards from the line of scrimmage, so that he will not be compelled to take too many backward steps in order to be six or seven yards from the line when he receives the pass.

In the parallel back formation, the backs being about four and a half yards from the line of scrimmage, the ball may be passed naturally to any of them. Immediately before the snap of the ball, the intending kicker takes two full steps backward, timing himself so that he will receive the pass as he completes this retrograde movement. He then has opportunity to take two steps forward in order to get up speed and kick naturally.

If the kicker is the fullback, his right halfback charges immediately for the defensive left tackle, assuming that the latter will be the most likely blocker of the punt. The left half charges for the right tackle, under a similar assumption with regard to him.

If the right halfback is kicking, the fullback, taking care not to interfere with the pass, charges the left tackle; the left halfback doing as before. If the left halfback is kicking, the fullback, first guarding against blocking the pass, assumes the left halfback's former duty, and charges the defensive right tackle; while the right halfback charges the defensive left tackle.

The kick should be made from a point four and one-half to five yards from the line of scrimmage. This renders very remote the possibility of a block by either of the defensive ends. Furthermore, the charge of the non-punting backs gives the play the appearance of a running attack or a trick play. And as both these backs charge well inside the defensive ends, the latter are immediately put upon their guard against the possibility of a play going just inside or possibly just outside of them. This further adds to the improbability that they will take any prominent part in blocking the kick.

This kick, to be blocked by the end, would necessitate too sharp an immediate charge by the latter into the backfield; and would expose him hopelessly to a run around his end. Even if he diagnosed the play in time and correctly, he would not dare to charge at an angle so narrow with respect to the line of scrimmage, and tempt the punter not to kick the ball, but to run around him.

As there is every indication to the defensive guards that a play is coming through one tackle or the other, the regular tight-line charge by the five men from tackle to tackle, substantially hitting the defensive center trio and then going down the field, is sufficient line protection on this kick. The defensive center, if on the line of scrimmage, is the only dangerous man, provided the halfbacks perform the simple duty of blocking the tackles or driving them outside. In case the well known tandem backfield formation is used, it would be advisable to make the pass to the last man in the tandem; the first man blocking the tackle on his side, the second man blocking the tackle on the other side.

The quarterback on this kick has a very important task. I have always used the play with the quarterback originally under center. I see no reason why it should fail in any way if he should happen to be one of a four-man backfield. This being a surprise formation, the quarter calls the substantial part of the signal numbers while standing in his position. As he begins the call of the sequence numbers containing the starting signal, he rushes toward the wide side of the field to a point approximately on the scrimmage line, without taking any chances, however, of being offside. He comes to a dead stop immediately before his call of the starting number itself, and charges down the field under the kick with the call of the starting number.

This gives the kicking team the advantage of an extra man to go immediately down the field. The danger of disaster to the team using the quick kick is very slight. The kicker, to be sure, should not kick a low ball; The defensive line, discovering late that there is nothing more serious on than a kick, and having been allowed to ooze through between the forwards who go down the field, will make a tardy attempt to block, but it should not be dangerous. If, on account of serious inferiority in the kicking team's line, it is considered specially dangerous to allow the line from left guard to right tackle to go down at once under the kick, there is at least the consolation that the left end and tackle, right end and quarterback have started immediately. Even in this case, the surprise feature of the kick, and the fact that, except on fourth down, there is seldom more than one receiver in the far back-field, are decisive points of superiority over the punt from regular formation.

I have said that even on fourth down this kick has its good features. I believe this to be true; but frankly, I have never so used it. A certain amount of excusable misapprehension would be experienced by the kicking team, due to the almost positive foreknowledge of the defense as to the nature of the play. This misapprehension is actually no greater than the defending team would experience seeing the attack lined up in any other than a decisive kick formation; yet the mental attitude of one's own team, facing a fourth down in the vicinity of its goal line, appears to be a sufficiently important factor to compel the use of the steady, settled kick formation under such conditions, with all defensive and offensive preparations carefully made before the ball is snapped. In other parts of the field, even on fourth downs, the surprise kick, with its alluring opportunities for trick plays, has its strong points. On other than fourth downs, with a good kicker, it is easily superior.

"A Good Kicker"
Unidentified Contributor

CHAPTER XXVIII: PUNTING ---
THE REGULAR FORMATION

For those who will have none of the quick kick there are several punt formations which might be called standard. The one best known calls for a kicker back in position, two backs forward in tandem on the right and one on the left. That is, the quarter does not remain under center. Of course, there are many excellent plays possible from this formation; especially if the man in the punter's position possesses the threats of accurate forward passing or known speed in running the ends. But here we limit ourselves to the kick itself, and the assignments of the whole team when a kick is in order.

It will be noted again that I have taken the quarterback away from center, and put him in one of the three positions mentioned to aid in the protection of the kicker. Take first the assignments of these three backfield men. The reason so many kicks are blocked by men who should be stopped by the protecting backs is very simple. The backs move from their positions prematurely. The single man on the left is assigned to block the right tackle. He is placed about two yards directly behind his own left tackle. The front man in the tandem on the right is placed in the same relative position behind his right tackle. The second man in the tandem is about a yard behind him, and his specific task is to block the left end. A better way to put it is as follows: the defensive guards in regular position and the center between them, or their equivalent, are included objectively in the close charge of the five offensive forwards from tackle to tackle. The first loose defensive man outside the charge of these five-line men must be blocked, if the kicker is to be given a fair opportunity. Therefore the first loose man outside the offensive left tackle must be taken by the single backfield man on the left of the kicker; and the first loose man on the outside of the offensive right tackle must be stopped by the first man in the tandem on the right of the kicker. The second loose man outside the right tackle must be managed by the second man in the tandem.

These three men, who must be prevented from getting at the kicker, are generally the tackles and the defensive left end; but this may not be so. For instance, the defensive right tackle may move out and the defensive quarter, having decided to take a chance, may come up to fill his space. Now, if the protecting back on the kicking team insists upon blocking the tackle, and him alone, the defensive quarter will go through with a fair chance to cover the kicker's leg. Or, the defensive quarter may go up outside of tackle on the other side, and if the second man in the tandem still undertakes to block the end, this new man, who is nearer the kicker, will go through without obstacle.

It is also possible that a team may split its line against very probable kicks. One big eleven for several years blocked a considerable number of seemingly inevitable or dangerous kicks by bunching guard tackle and end as close together as they conveniently could run outside of the offensive tackle, and leaving the center and defensive quarter alone in the middle of the line to defend as best they could against an improbable thrust in that direction. Plainly these two men, against a well directed center attack, would be ineffective. Their danger materialized in 1911, and nearly cost this team one of its big games, when opponents on a place-kick formation, let the ball be snapped to the pretended placekicker direct, instead of to the kneeling quarter, who was supposed to place and hold it. The runner dashed through center without serious opposition except by the fullback. No team should go on the field without such a play.

The way to manage kick formations is to call: "place kick formation," "drop kick formation," "punt formation." Announce them thus. Give your team plenty of time to form, taking plenty of time yourself to size up the positions assumed by the defense. Then give your signal. Having a play corrective of any tendency opponents may show to split their line, your team will find itself at no disadvantage if that formation does appear.

The punter on any of the standard kick formations should retire at least ten yards from the ball, and he should be preferably ten yards back from the spot of the snap when he makes his kick, or twelve yards originally. The extra two yards is an important item in giving the line its opportunity to get down the field. And, of course, it is also so much additional protection against blocking.

The offensive ends must make certain that they are in a position to get away immediately without the slightest interference. If possible, they should maintain their regular position in offensive attack, which, as elsewhere stated, gives them considerable latitude; they being instructed to shift in and out continually, in order that they may be able to assume the especially desirable position when the attack depends particularly upon their ability to block the tackle. Here the chances are that the tackle will be glad to let the end alone, thereby increasing his own opportunity to block the kick. If the end is forced to go outside of the tackle, he should wait until the last possible moment before so doing.

The end's necessity of securing freedom of choice and action is one of the strongest reasons for continuing to use a starting signal in case of a punt. Then the end can know to a fraction of a second when the snap of the ball is to occur; and, if the tackle is especially persistent, he can jump away from him in a safe position and be barely set in time for his start down the field.

Usually the defensive tackle is glad to let him alone, and to be let alone, in order to give his entire attention to the more important mission of blocking the kick.

The rest of the line from tackle to tackle is in close formation, and if there is any slight distance between individuals, in order not to create too great a certainty of a kick, or in order to include the defensive trio or duo (in case one of the three drops back), they must make a converging charge. No one must be allowed to break through. The kicker, if his hands are in position to receive the pass, should specially guard against closing his fists and opening them on the snap number. Plainly this is too much help to give the enemy. Now we are ready for the snap number. It is called. The ball is on its way to the fullback.

The entire line of seven men is on its way, the rushline from tackle to tackle charging with a tendency toward convergence, and striking hard, with head and shoulders, the central opposition; then sliding off these opponents, the center rush continuing straight down the field until he receives the necessary intelligence; guards and tackles, now separated enough to have free movement, also waiting for further enlightenment; ends charging straight for the defensive halfbacks, under no circumstances slowing down their utmost speed. For it is the end who hesitates that is broken down by an opponent. Every man on the rushline has three instinctive thoughts in mind. One, to dodge the interferers, without slowing down. Two, to listen for warnings from the kicker as to the direction of the kick.

Three, to watch the action of the opponents down the field, in order to pass judgment (and act accordingly) without wasting time in looking up for the ball, as to the probable distance and direction of the kick. Having determined the probable landing place of the punt, the center changes his course and heads for the catcher. The entire line also considers the catcher as the basis for general direction; but spreads slightly, like a fan, with the idea of enmeshing him with seven men instead of two or three.

The ends now charge in a direction slightly outside the receiver. They continue to advance outside of him until judgment tells them that they can reach him direct. The forwards will not all arrive together, nor will they arrive in the shape of a perfect fan; but as they approach the catcher they converge upon him, guards, tackles and center making him their direct target, while the ends continue to keep on the outside as long as doubt exists as to their ability to reach him. But each man should be filled with the firm intention to take a hard drive at the receiver, whether he misses him or not. In going down under kicks it is not the man who misses his tackle who should receive censure, but the man who stays on his feet, watching the gyrations of his would-be prey until the latter finally sifts past him and breaks into the open. In case either tackle discovers that his end has been taken down, he must change direction and play his man a little wider than before. In fact, the idea of fan-like convergence must be kept in mind. This is the only way to pull down without chance of escape a shifty, fast-dodging receiver. Do not let him keep his poise. So long as he does, he is dangerous. Drive him precipitately from the hand tackle of the first and perhaps the second man into the arms of the third. So long as he can dance he is never down.

We must now return to the busy backfield. The three protecting backs, with open eyes and quiet intelligence, are poised; calmly braced, knowing the positive line of attack that their individual adversaries must take, if any one of them is to be in time to block the kick. Each knows that if his individual prey assumes a false direction it is nothing more than a stall, to draw him off balance, in order that the would-be blocker may dodge immediately back into his proper line of approach with the minimum waste of time.

Instead, the protector waits until the last possible instant, and then coolly picking his direction, and with all his energy, crashes hard and fast with head and shoulders and body following into his advancing opponent. If this is done as here stated, the punt goes on its way. If any one of the three misses his man, it is needless and often worse than useless to chase him, at least with any idea of restoring the opportunity. In case of a bad pass, lost or fumbled by the kicker, he announces to his mates in the back-field his predicament by the immediate cry of "Ball."

In this case, whether the protectors of the kicker have blocked their men or not, it is their plain duty to rush to his aid; always ready by blocking to prevent an opponent getting the ball, unless positive of a better solution, to wit, ability to recover the pigskin by out-speeding the others. Returning now to the point where the charging enemy has been blocked or missed, there having been no indication but that the ball has been properly received and kicked, the protectors have two immediate thoughts in mind. One, to get down the field at once. Two, to see with their own eyes the distance and direction of the kick. The same thoughts should now be in the mind of the kicker. He has called in his clearest, loudest tones the direction of the kick: "Center!" "Left!" "Right!"

All the backs, kicker included, should materially help, if it is physically possible, in the event of a successful nm-back of the kick.

In the case of a particularly poor kick, to the left or right, these four men become the last reserve. If they do not operate immediately and effectively, the milk is spilled. Referring for a moment to the protector who has failed to block his man, it is a question whether he should follow out the instructions just given, applying to the man who has blocked his opponent, or whether he should rally to the kicker, not with the hopeless idea of overtaking the blocker, and blocking the kick himself, if particularly unlucky or clumsy, but with the idea in mind to engage in the race for the ball if the kick is blocked. The decision in this matter must defend upon the known conditions, namely, the speed of the eluding blocker, the direction taken by him, and the further probability of his being able to block the kick, having in mind the skill and speed of the kicker. The back's good judgment must be exercised according to circumstances.

CHAPTER XXIX: PUNTING --- BLOCK KICKS --- THE SPIRAL

More kicks are blocked through the vanity or over-eagerness of forwards who are anxious to get down the field and shine in the open than through poor passing or slow handling. The left tackle of the punting team no longer leads the linemen down the field. Instead, the whole line from tackle to tackle is supposed to make its charges as a solid wall, taking out everything that is in a bumpable position. After bumping and delaying the defensive center trio, the linemen slide off from these contacts and go on down the field. The better lines have been specializing intensively on going down under kicks. There is enough pride, conceit or ambition in most forwards to induce them to go down as fast as they can, to do something brilliant in the open field.

The ambitious forward, however, will thus sometimes take too many chances, and give a crafty defending lineman a chance to sift through fast and block a kick. In the long run, right guards have blocked many kicks because left tackles, with brilliant down-the-field reputations to sustain, have made haste to depart, leaving the guard to his own devices. But the whole blocking system goes to smash if the tackle jumps away and leaves the guard loose.

One of the more effective methods of blocking kicks is to inject an extra man into the line. Some teams accomplish the same purpose, that of gaining additional strength which cannot be covered, by splitting the defensive line; trusting, that the kicking team will be so foolish as to insist upon punting, instead of running the ball through the thin center of the line.

Probably the worst thing that can happen to spoil a kick is to have the right tackle, purposely avoiding the left guard, start on his way down the field in all his eagerness or selfishness. The guard has naturally taken a position almost directly in front of the right tackle. In fact, it is well worth while and particularly clever on the part of the left guard who intends sometime during the game to block a kick, to make no pretense of attempting to block two or three, but to spend all his time interfering with the tackle's getaway. Whereupon the tackle, being hard put to it to figure in the down-the-field work, and noting that the guard is making no effort to block the kick, soon decides in his simplicity that his first main effort must be to evade this guard.

He is now properly baited, and the guard awaits his next opportunity. With a great demonstration before the snapping of the ball, he intimates to his tackle adversary that this particular time he is going to stop him completely in his tracks. The ball sails back to the kicker. The right tackle makes a terrific jump, in the only open direction left to him, outside the defensive guard. Not at all strangely, he finds himself free to go; for the guard suddenly ceases his blocking activities, and charges point-blank through the space the tackle has just left. Having probably the shortest route to the kicker's foot of any man along the entire defensive line, he continues with all his speed for the fullback's kicking leg and jumps high and squarely into the air, with arms raised high and hands wide open. The kick is blocked, and the game perhaps lost, through the error of the kicker's right tackle. We read frequently of the guard who bursts through the opposing line and blocks a kick. Here is the inside story of that occurrence. In conclusion it should be stated that if the tackles never get down the field in time to take part in bringing down the receiver of the kick, they must at least pound and restrain the guards.

It may be questioned, why cannot one of the backs stop the guard. The answer is that he could if he knew the guard was to be left uncovered. He has his plain duty marked out for him. If the backfield man assigned to stop the tackle, seeing the new danger, should shift and block the guard, the tackle's menace would become almost as great.

There is no excuse for the blocking of a kick where the pass is good, the individuals of the team properly complete their assignments and the kicker is reasonably fast in getting the ball away. The spiral pass has lessened the likelihood that a kick can be blocked, and if, in addition, the punter stands a dozen yards from the scrimmage line, a perfect pass, perfectly handled and booted, could hardly be blocked by an unopposed sprinter in track shoes and costume. Yet kicks are blocked occasionally, and occasionally will be. The effort is worth making; although there is no reason why a defensive line should not know not only the theory of blocking kicks, but also the technique of blocking lines that are going down under kicks. A decisive runback of a kick may turn the tide in a game, and is a very disturbing incident for the team on the wrong end.

If the particularly fast, dangerous man can be prevented from going down the field, it may be worth while for his opposite to disdain the blocking of the kick. If the line is particularly tight, the three center men of the defense can materially interfere with the charge of this line down the field, provided they elect to so do instead of attempting to block the kick.

There are several theories of punting, including, of course, the pass for the punt. All that a punter can be expected to do, if not rushed, is to punt the ball in the general direction he intended. Punting in a game and punting in practice are two entirely different things. Against a good team the punter will have to hurry. In order to get accurate direction the ball must be dropped accurately, and the foot must be swung against the ball accurately.

There will be a slight variation in both the dropping of the ball, and the meeting of the ball with the foot, on almost every kick. Either will be sufficient to thwart the punter in any intended specific deflection. I will not say that no punter has ever placed a kick while under pressure; for in a general sense of direction I have seen it done with a fair degree of frequency. But when we hear of a punter making successfully a forty-yard or a fifty-yard kick, with the calculated intention of having it cross the sideline at the five-yard mark, the statement never fails to excite considerable skepticism among those who have observed the vagaries of the prolate spheroid when booted.

A coach shows his backs his style, and there are many styles. The theory of distance, whether you kick a spiral or not, is in the drive and follow through, just as in golf. If the kicker who comes to you ready made is getting satisfactory results in his own style, it is seldom advisable to alter it. If his work is already good he is bound to improve it, and any coach is satisfied with a good, fast kicker. Oftentimes an extremely long kick has operated against the kicker. It is extremely difficult to regulate the length of the punt when the kicker is under fire; and beside the undesirable possibility of a touchback resulting from a long kick, we have the even more dangerous condition which exists when the kicks are too long to be covered.

The moral is that kicks of moderate length, covered every time, are eminently satisfactory.

Briefly, there are three generally accepted styles of punting. Least often seen is the kick which begins with the kicker holding the ball very low, about two feet from the ground; the player being actually in a crouched position. The only apparent advantages of this style are increased accuracy in dropping the ball, and the meeting of the ball with the foot more precisely as intended. It has been very ably followed by several fairly prominent kickers, and with good results. But unless the man came to me with this style well developed, I should not be in favor of it. It generally yields a low kick, with a consequent increased danger that it may be blocked. The distance of flight is seldom as great as other styles produce. But it does have the advantage that, if not caught on the fly, the ball has a long roll and carry, and is difficult to handle, as all rolling, bounding balls ever are.

The other extreme, used by many of the best kickers of recent years, is the kick produced by holding the ball very high and dropping it to meet a long swinging drive, which is carried through to the envy of the high kicker of the older days, who used to practice on a tambourine. This style yields a very high kick, of tremendous power, and when carried through accurately the ball is given a slightly spiral effect. But the spiral effect soon wears off, and the ball drops dead and straight, and so becomes very difficult to handle.

In both of these styles the swing of the leg is very nearly straight, which is sufficient of itself to lessen any tendency toward a pronounced spiral.

The third style, and to me the preferable one, begins by holding the ball at a height even with the chest, slightly to the side of the body; the end pointing in the direction intended for the kick, and slightly lowered in order to fit the ball to the instep more perfectly when dropped. The ball really lies on the right hand, string up, steadied with the fingers of the left hand; held at full reach well outside the kicker's leg; released by dropping the hand after the last step is completed, and met slightly on the outside of the instep. The toes are extended downward, the knee locked and the leg rigid. Impetus is given by the circular swing which is necessitated by the dropping of the ball in the position as indicated. The carry-through will bring the foot level with the left shoulder, the toe pointing decidedly to the left. The swing is such that were the ball missed the kicker would describe almost a complete revolution, with his left foot as an axis. The ball should be dropped as far forward as it is possible to drop it and still fulfil the conditions outlined, because the greater the extension of the leg, the greater the speed of the movement and the distance acquired. This kick is not difficult to learn, and gives a beautiful cut, productive of a spiral that will bore its way through a hurricane.

In addition to being the best kick against the wind, this particular punt gives superior results with a wet ball or on a slippery field, the kicker in the latter case having less liability or sensation of losing his footing and toppling over backward.

The kicker, as well as the forward passer, must always be ready for quick reverses. A badly misdirected kick to the side, like a forward pass of the same kind, demands decisive action, as the kicker or passer is usually the last man in the backfield when the mishap occurs.

Very weighty arguments for the use of the rhythmatic starting signal are found in the fact that the ends are able to get away more quickly under punts when that signal is used. They know that the ball is going to be kicked. They have formed their complete plan of getting down the field, and now they can await the starting signal with the assurance that they are to receive a liberal, although absolutely legal, start. This should be cause for increased confidence on their part, and confidence, surely, is one of the greatest assets to an end going down under kicks.

This same benefit accrues to the entire rushline, with the additional slight though very important advantage that the kicker has a small additional fraction of a second in which to get the ball away. When one considers that a ball kicked one and four-fifths seconds after the center moves his hands to pass in the ordinary kick formation is considered perfectly safe, provided it rises at a reasonable angle of departure, whereas a punt delayed for two and one-fifth seconds should be blocked, it will be seen how precious are the fractions of a second.

If any man other than the captain and the quarterback is entitled to speak his mind on the football field and assert his own individuality, that man is the punter. Entirely on a co-operative basis, he should work things out with his field general. Thus: "Tom, keep the wind in mind. I'm here to kick whenever you say, but I don't want to kick out of bounds ten yards from the scrimmage line. I want to have freedom to kick in my natural position." Or: "This is the day for high punts if I want to get distance. I find the wind is a good deal stronger up above. So give me plenty of room. You know me, Al."

A team loves to feel that it has a quarterback who can run the game. The players are also especially pleased with the knowledge that the captain is listening to every signal, though he almost never enters into the selection of plays, and that if he does intervene, he will come mighty near to being right. Also the thought is very pleasant and reassuring that the punter's kicks are being manipulated not only in accordance with the best judgment of the punter, but in complete accord with the intent of both quarterback and captain. "Now," say the other men on the team, "we are able and ready to do the rest."

CHAPTER XXX: PUNTING --- THE RUNBACK

The runback of a kick depends almost entirely on the individual skill of the receiver, against a strong offensive team. There was a time, not many years ago, when all the receiver had to think about, immediately on catching the ball, was one end, or perhaps two. On the better teams the left tackle might also be a factor. These being the immediate arrivals, great efforts were made to erase them from the landscape. But, nowadays, with the strong tendency and great improvement of teams in getting a large part of the rushline down under kicks immediately, the job of protection by the receiving team has assumed practically impossible proportions; with the unfortunate result that ends are now able to go down the field with much less serious opposition than formerly. It is not uncommon, in fact, and incidentally it is a delight, to see some big guard or center performing the unwelcomed attention of slapping the receiver to the ground. Certain it is that the player who hopes to run back a kick must be ready to evade four or five tacklers, unless he is fortunate enough to catch the ball on the dead run off to the side where his opponents cannot cover him properly.

With the forward passing game developed as it is, it is not feasible to give the receiver more than one helper. The helper should be the best punt-catcher of the three secondary defense backs. Contrary to the general impression, there are very few punters who can place the punt with any degree of accuracy. I now refer to the punter in his big games, and all games should be played on the same system as the big games. The punter of the team which is up against its equal usually has pretty nearly all he can manage to get his punt away. A right-legged kicker who has instructions to kick to the wide side of the field when that side is on his right, is very fortunate in the assistance given him by his protective backs if he has time enough to turn and kick directly in line with the tackle and end who are charging in to block. The same thing is substantially true if the same kicker attempts to kick to the left of the field. Ordinarily, the defensive right end has little opportunity to block the kick, but that opportunity is increased if the kicker makes a pronounced turn; to say nothing of the right tackle. In other words, the kicker is generally forced by a good defensive team to use the less dangerous space directly in front of him to get his kicks away, rather than to swing to left or right.

If, as sometimes happens, however, a team finds itself up against a kicker who can place his punts with a fair degree of accuracy, the defensive fullback should play the wide side of the field. The second man who is sent back should take the center of the field, slightly to the narrow side. But if the punter, either because of strong defensive charging, or his inability, does not place his punts, then the defensive fullback should defend the general center zone, with the second man protecting on the wide side of the field.

I have often heard and read of one back or the other playing the short side of the field, but have never been able to arrive at a safe conclusion as to what is meant by it. I recall a big game, a few years ago, in which one of the contesting teams played the short side of the field on the kicker's right. The kicker almost invariably throughout the game kicked well over the short-field player, at the expense to the latter's team of perhaps one hundred yards, with the additional penalty that the chances of runbacks were practically eliminated. No punter, with the rules as they are, intends to kick short, except the outside kick or where a long kick would result in a touchback. The proper position for the fullback and his helper to assume are those which best cover the kicking field.

If the man who goes back to assist is one of the defensive half-backs, the defensive quarter of course takes his place. If there is still danger, on account of the position of the kicking team, of a forward pass, one of the center trio falls back into the defensive quarterback's position. A second member of the center trio assumes a position where he can keep watch over the offensive quarterback, if the latter maintains his position under center. If a punt is a practical certainty, either because of the down or the position of the offensive team, the center remains in the line.

The defensive fullback's regular position is twenty-five yards from scrimmage line, until he discovers that opponents have a kick from running formation which he cannot handle at that distance. In this case he increases his distance to thirty yards, which is also his distance on kick formations against average kickers and under normal conditions of wind and sun. His helper should play approximately the same distance from the line. If alone in the backfield, the fullback should incline toward the center of the field. If the ball is being scrimmaged fifteen yards from the sideline, after going out of bounds, the fullback should play twenty-five to thirty yards from the sidelines. As the distance to his own goal line diminishes, the defensive fullback's position must be governed by the same considerations as before. He must be able to defend against forward passes or long runs on either side, but his liability against long punts decreases as the distance shortens. If his team is defending, for instance, on the twenty-yard line, he would be likely to play no wider than his own end on the inside of the field, and would stand, perhaps, on the five-yard line. He takes the nearest central spot to all the things which may happen which are in his line and which he can get.

As the attack nears the goal line, the defensive fullback's duties merge into halfback duties or even into rushline forward duties. Many teams strengthen the line by injecting into it their heaviest back when driven within the fifteen-yard mark. The three remaining backs defend against forward passes, and also back up the line. The line should not be spread when reinforced. Instead, the spaces are tightened. Against a team kicking out from behind or near its own goal line it is also quite usual to put the heaviest back in the line, to increase the chances of blocking the kick. If the extra man is fast, he can hurry the kicker, at least, by a change from just outside right tackle; his chances being considerably better than those of the right end, who is much farther out. The single man defending on the kicker's left, especially if required to swing out from the quarterback's position to block, is easy to avoid. On the other side of the line, with two protectors and three blockers going in, there is usually too much congestion to give the extra fast man full scope.

One reads many treatises and sees much practice undertaken with a view to instructing and developing the second backfield receiver in order that he may be of the greatest possible help to his mate who is catching, or has just caught the ball. Generally the instruction is along the line that the former should direct the catcher as to the better direction to take; with some advice as to the protection to be given on the runback. You will probably agree with me that this generally results in the leader starting away just in time to have his teammate picked up by a sure tackier.

The man who is advised as to his direction by another is by no means as capable of warding off trouble as the one who, having caught the ball, takes as much time as the circumstances allow, and then chooses his own path. In the former case the receiver knows that he has turned himself and his judgment over to another. He is divided between his attempt to follow his teammate and his desire to bolt on his account. I have never yet seen an interferer select a path straight up the field, where the runner would be behind him. At the time when he chooses the course, which almost inevitably is to left or right, the opponents are nearly upon him and the catcher. Naturally, then, his start, either to left or right, leaves his runner entirely exposed, and the latter's aspirations are nipped in the bud. Where, then, is the protector going to run, if he runs at all? Naturally and logically, in a forward course, to all intents and purposes straight up the field.

What is he to do, if he wishes to give the best possible protection to the runner? Unquestionably he must bring down or block successfully the most dangerous man of those in his path. Probably he will have very little opportunity to go forward any great distance. If he blocks one determined tackier, whether by running into him and keeping his own feet, or by throwing his body across him, it matters little. In either case, he will be left so far behind as to be of little further help to his partner. By all means he should keep his feet if he can.

He might be able, by very slight blocking, sensing the position of his teammate, and knowing the latter's ability to avoid difficulties, to save him in the first instance, and even to render him further assistance. This settles down to a question of the interferer's own skill and judgment. But every consideration leads us back to the one main idea, which is that the second man in the backfield renders his best assistance by getting to the catcher, on either side, in time to assist in the receiving of the ball if fumbled, and, if the ball is caught, by eliminating the first man down the field who could spoil the runback if let alone. By all means let him take out two or three of them if possible, but it is generally the case that he can only feature and function once on each kick.

Many other ideas have been tried, such as instructing the other secondary defense men to retire into the backfield, as soon as satisfied that the ball has been or will be kicked, there to put up their battle in defense of the catcher. This is excellent in theory, but in practice the ends and other members of the kicker's side have reached these retreating halfbacks about the time the ball is punted. Usually they find the retirement of the defensive backs more agreeable to them than immediate opposition would be. The ends, at least, welcome a trial of speed under these conditions. If the backs keep pace with the ends they only help to create a barrier against the punt-catcher, who finds it almost as difficult to dodge friend as foe.

The catcher's best path usually is straight up the field. It is better to take a chance with the center and guards than with the supposedly more accurate tackles and ends. The line is running down to cover the field. Clever dodging of one or two men where the line is thinnest may mean the equivalent of dodging the entire line.

If the advancing tacklers have already converged upon the catcher, with the ends coming slightly from the outside and the others well bunched, the chances at the center are probably hopeless. There is only one dodge in this case, and only one question, whether to the right or the left; the best of a bad lot. But I have seen one man who could side-step the tackle, jump back into the spot the tackle had just left, thus avoiding the end, and go! We may not see another Thorpe in the immediate future, but it is certain that experienced punt-catchers will endeavor more and more to protect themselves by the use of stratagem.

And in this connection, there is another way to raise consternation and havoc with the opposing team, and that is for the punt receiver to pretend that he awaits the ball where he is standing or dancing about, when actually the ball is descending rapidly several yards ahead, where he intends to take it presently by a sudden sprint. Another possible, although seldom effective deception is for the helper to dance under an imaginary ball, while the receiver-to-be stands in nonchalant indifference, but ready to tuck away the real ball, which is fast descending.

Or the helper may, in another case, cut across suddenly in front of his partner and take the ball on the dead run, at the last possible instant. Any of these ruses may cause the down-the-field players to be penalized for interference. In the first case there is also a very good chance that the rushline may overrun the ball if the kick be short or high, despite the loud warnings of the fullback. It is one of the nerviest plays in football.

Of course, the backfield receivers will soon learn the caliber and ability of the opposing rushline in its down-the-field work. They will sense the amount of instruction opponents have had or been able to absorb, and will find out the weakness of their formation. If the ends are playing it too safe, coming down too wide in order to keep on the outside, with a view to preventing a runback along either wing, this gives the catcher his best chance to do his dodging around the tackle and end zone, as the end is likely to be late, and the distance between him and his tackle too great.

On the other hand, if the formation comes down well, with the field immediately in front properly covered, to attempt a wide detour at either end generally amounts to a guarantee against running back the kick. If his teammate in the far backfield can take down a determined looking character immediately in front, this leaves the catcher a pretty fair space through which to attempt his runback. If the line is badly spread and ragged, though the ends are in a formidable position, the straight course is again the better. And always, when in doubt, take the direct course. Every yard covered is a yard saved, and one successful dodge may mean a long gain.

The job of the other two backs should be to take out the ends. They should be carefully instructed and given practice in this very difficult part of the game. The ends are probably fast, and probably excellent tacklers. They are also on the extremities of the rushline going down, and if removed by the backs it would open the sides of the field to the punt-catcher. The most important one word of instruction to give these backs, by way of teaching them the blocking of ends, is never to allow the ends to get directly in front of them. Each should step to one side, and keep to one side, of the end, so that the latter has only a single direction in which to elude blocking. Having allowed him to get close enough so that he must now attempt to pass on the side which he has been forced to select, the back should make his drive for the spot where he knows his speed will be sufficient to meet his man, throwing his body with all the slam and speed possible across the end's upper legs. He need not be too much discouraged if he misses him, as he has at least driven him into making a wider detour than intended, causing him to be late down the field; beside filling him with an extra bit of worry and uncertainty for his next trip. If you do not make a man worry he seldom has much to worry about. Next time, very likely, the back will get the end.

Fair-catching of punts may be ordered by a coach in a specific game or for a special reason; but he seldom issues such instructions without considerable reluctance. The practice savors so little of fighting football that the mental effect of it on both teams is apt to be as bad as a mishandled kick. In theory, the team going down under kicks tends to relax its efforts, and thus provide an opportunity when the ball is fair-caught repeatedly. Actually, the enthusiasm of such a team increases. The players, feeling that they are forcing their opponents into an admission of weakness, and also that they are preventing any return of the ball, seem to charge faster and faster on every succeeding punt. It is also argued that the kicker's side can eventually be baited into an interference with a fair catch; but although the most expert of players will pull an occasional "bone," this particular offense is usually the last that a well-coached team will commit.

The receiver is justified in attempting a fair catch when he intends to try a free kick; in the case of a high and short, or a higher and longer, kick, which finds him closely surrounded and enveloped by opponents in force; and seldom, if ever, otherwise, unless specially commanded. It is better to play the ball on the bound than to make a fair catch because of fear, when under ordinary pressure; and in case of a very short kick it is nearly always good policy to let the ball bound, unless certain of the opponents are on side.

When the signal is given for a fair catch, the first arrival down the field should remain close to the receiver, to recover a fumble or to block him if he fumbles, thus preventing his recovery of the ball. Later arrivals should be alert for a possible loose ball. Fair-catchers should be warned against old-fashioned denting the ground with the heels so that the restraining mark thus made becomes indeed a restraint upon them to such an extent that they cannot manage themselves or recover balance. Teach them to stand naturally and they will not need even the two steps allowed by the rule.

CHAPTER XXXI: PUNTING --- DROP KICK AND PLACEMENT KICK

The starting signal, though admirable for punts, should not be used, except for some especially important reason, in the case of drop or place kicks. These kicks are, in comparison with punts, so seldom called for, and have generally so important a specific bearing on the outcome of the game that the kicker's mental attitude is considerably different. His apprehensions as to blocking are more acute, and it is more essential for his peace of mind and assurance that he take plenty of time and receive the pass only when he has signified his preparedness.

Furthermore, the abominable custom on many teams of the kicker opening his hands as the signal for the pass precipitates an immediate charge by the defensive team which often gets by the officials, though slightly offside, and frequently results in the blocking of the attempted kick. It may be argued that this signal might be used, contrary to the rules, for the purpose of drawing the defensive team offside; but the great point in the matter is this, if the offensive team really desires to score by the drop kick or placement route, it surely does not care to take a chance on the opponents' offside, with a possible blocking of the attempt as a result, as well as the uncertainty as to the umpire's decision on the offside.

The best scheme to follow in case of a try at a field goal is for the kicker, having made full preparations to receive the pass, to say to the center something along this line: "All right. Jack, any time you're ready I am." This speech has its psychological effect upon the center rush, as well as a possible effect upon the defense. At any rate, it gives the defensive team no specific advance information as to the pass. The center then passes the ball when ready; advisedly, of course, as soon as possible after the notice given him by the kicker; in order that there may be no undue tension caused by delay. In this case there is no great disadvantage to the kicker's side resulting from its being compelled to watch for the snap of the ball; for the reason that, except for the ends, the first move by the offense is a defensive one: protection for the kicker. This does not mean that the line should not charge. It does charge, just as on a punt. The old theory of a brace is discarded, as the charge is a better brace. But there is not that extreme necessity of getting down the field immediately, in the great majority of placement or drop kicks; for it is seldom that the kick, if not blocked, fails to result in a touchback, if not in a goal. Therefore, the rushline can afford to block more solidly, and a little longer, before going down under the kick.

There is now no excuse whatever for the selfish or over-zealous tackle, who leaves the opposing guard while the latter has still the remotest chance to block the try at goal.

Even the end plays a slightly different part in this phase of the kicking game than he would under a punt. As a special precaution against a poor attempt, especially a wide kick which does not go into touch, he must go down the field at once; but his position when the ball is snapped is close to his tackle; whereas he has some power of selection on punt formations. His charge now is directed at the side of the defensive tackle's body nearer the ball; assuming, of course, that the tackle is not a yard or more outside the end, in which case the latter does not have to bother with him at all. This charge at the side of the tackle's body nearest the center is made to force the tackle to avoid the end, by charging around him, thus making his path to the kicker so much the longer and less direct.

Under this system of protection, the blocking of tries at goal should be next to impossible. Even a line of very moderate strength should be able to prevent a direct block by one of the opposing center trio. Its charge, with the slight exceptions noted, is similar to its charge on a punt; but the closer to the goal line when the try at goal is attempted, the greater should be the spread of the line after its initial charge. The ends having charged straight with their tackles, and staying with the line a moment longer than on a punt, are likely to be a trifle late in their down-the-field effort to prevent a possible runback.

The nearer or the farther from the scrimmage line that a drop or place kick can be delivered with sufficient height to clear the rushlines, the less liability of a block. A passer who could deliver a fast spiral to a kicker twenty yards away would assure absolutely the safety of any kick directed high enough in the air to clear a cross-bar. But the longer the pass the greater the danger that it may miscarry; the longer, too, the distance required of the kicker. At fifteen yards the danger that a try at goal may be blocked begins to be felt. At eight yards the danger probably is greatest, from that surge of blockers from the wings which, and which only, if his line be sound and properly coached, the kicker has to fear. Nearer than that, the danger of kicking into one's own line or opponents' increases directly just as the danger of a block from the sides decreases.

And this is why the placement kick is much less dangerous than the drop-kick close to the scrimmage line. Few drop-kickers dare attempt their specialty seven yards from scrimmage; fair placement kickers can attempt theirs from five. The angle of departure can always be controlled in the place-kick; the kicker needs no more than a third of the accuracy required of a drop-kicker in this respect, and in other respects also. The nearer to the scrimmage line the more nearly impossible the detour that the wingmen must describe in order to arrive in front of the kicker's toe; the more effective the protection given by the backs, who increase the distance of that detour, and the shorter the time in which the defense can operate.

"Future Players"
Harris & Ewing

And the place-kick is much the faster of the two; the ball is already kicked when a drop-kicker would still be turning it in his hands to avoid the lacing. At seven yards or less from the scrimmage line, the defensive tackles, practically speaking, are the only opponents who could block the kick. The ends are too far away. To block, they must take the same paths as the tackles;

in other words, they must follow the tackles if the latter charge through in time, or collide with them if the latter are late. Moreover, an end would hardly dare to charge so close to the line of scrimmage as to block the kick he must do. If he did, he would be wholly at the mercy of a trick play around him.

It is not too difficult to understand why white sheep eat more hay than black ones. But the explanation throws no light on their respective merits as sheep. Similarly vague is the equally unchallenged statement that more scores in football are made by drop-kickers than by placement-kickers. This is unquestionably true, but it fails to compromise my contention that the placement kick is surer than the drop kick; that it is quicker, easier, and less likely to be blocked.

There are a dozen drop-kickers for every placekicker. But this, after all, is easy to understand. Given a boy and a football, and a few newspaper headlines for romantic inspiration, a tree or the side of a barn for a goal, and the development of drop-kickers may begin very early in life.

The place-kick, on the other hand, involves the participation of an assistant whose comparatively inglorious role may breed boredom, rebellion even. The drop-kicker may drop-kick all day. It is not so easy for him to find the willing slave who is content all day to poise and steady the ball. Moreover, in games, the holder of the ball, though his part in the performance may be comparatively insignificant, shares not a little in the credit of achievement. To be sure, the center who passes the ball deserves a third share in that credit; but centers, from of old, are hardened and accustomed to neglect and oblivion. [Walter] Eckersall of Chicago twice kicked five field goals in one game, so history records. History makes no special mention of the centers who passed to him. Neither was the name of the boy who poised the ball considered worthy of record in the case of Alfred Griggs, a California schoolboy credited with fifteen goals from placement in a single game.

But, even so, drop-kickers get a very special thrill out of the orig-inality and uniqueness of their single-handed, or rather single-footed, achievements; whereas the placekicker, while neglecting as a matter of course the center's claims to recognition, is com-pelled to admit after the game that he who caught, placed and poised the ball also did well.

This individual catches and places the ball upright, with scarcely more than a single motion, at the same time revolving it so that the lacing is on the side farthest from the kicker. The placer should have plenty of practice with the center in receiv-ing the pass while in a kneeling position and in placing the ball accurately and straight up on a smooth spot previously selected and indicated to the kicker. The ball is held firmly in place by the finger tips of either hand.

It may be argued that the placement kick seems to involve the accuracy of two men instead of one only; but the placer need not be a wonder. If he be the quarterback, as probably is the case, he is already well accustomed to the handling of the ball from center; while the actual placing of the ball is an exceedingly simple assignment. The kicker, knowing precisely where the ball is to be placed, locates himself where a line from his advancing toe through the center of the ball will bisect the goal, if there is no wind. Like the drop-kicker, he must calculate the speed of his kick and its height, and make proper allowance for the wind. But his advantage over the drop-kicker in ability to control and regu-late the direction and the angle of departure is positive. Prompt and decisive elevation on placement kicks can be acquired by anybody. Many drop-kicks, especially if driven hard in order to obtain distance, leave the ground at a low angle, and would assur-edly strike one rushline or the other if kicked from five, or even seven, yards behind center.

The drop-kicker comes to the coach all made, almost invari-ably. His specialty involves the utmost accuracy, the result of constant practice, but there are almost as many ways to execute the kick as there are drop-kickers. Some drop the ball, some actually throw it to the ground. Some meet the ball with the toe, some with the instep and not a few with the shin-bone. Probably there have been very few successful college drop-kickers who were not proficient as schoolboys. It is part of their special distinction that they develop themselves. Early in life they get acquainted with their own mannerisms, and practice their kicks a thousand times. If you want to prove it, leave a few loose footballs around during practice for the students and town boys to amuse themselves withal. You will discover that you have more drop-kickers in your student-body than you have men on the squad, and also that the first thing a small boy does, when given possession of a football, is to inaugurate his career as a drop-kicker — unless he makes up his mind, owing to sloth and general disability, that he is going to be a guard.

Drop-kickers attach themselves to football squads, and are retained even when the team has an excellent place kicker; on the theory, never adequately proven or disproven, that for long distances the drop kick is the surer. There is also the idea that long drop-kicks may be used instead of punts.

Most coaches secretly abhor both drop and place kickers, in the belief that to put reliance in them is a weakening influence upon the rushing spirit of the team; an influence which may eventually force a team to depend upon the method of scoring which they provide. Many a high-class drop and place kicker has been graduated without attaining great reputation in football, although a member of the squad every season of his eligible career, because he has not had sufficiently numerous opportunities to display his consistent ability, the spirit and inclination of his teams having been to score touchdowns.

CHAPTER XXXII: KICK-OFF AND THE RUNBACK

Some of the best kickers build a very high tee for their kick-off. They have established the very good habit of swinging with the knee locked; and the left foot on the last step before the kick-off is placed considerably farther from the ball than if the ball were placed on a low tee. This necessitates a great extension of the right toe, in order to meet the ball. Kicking in this position, with the leg in the condition stated, the high tee is necessary, or the cleats of the right shoe would catch in the turf as the kicking leg passes the other.

On the other hand, many of the long-distance kickers operate with not much more in the way of a tee than a few grains of sand. They rely on their speed to put the power behind the ball. The left foot, before the kick is made, is very close to the ball. This kick-off is generally best achieved by the speedy, wiry player. It may be noted frequently that the kicker experiences practically no difficulty in maintaining his speed without a break; whereas the kicker with the long, pendulum-like leg-drive is usually brought to a stop by the act of kicking, and, if required to go down the field, is given a bad handicap. The coach is satisfied with either type of kicker if he can boot the ball into touch.

On the kick-off, the kicking team should line up not according to the general custom, with the men covering the entire width of the field. There is no justification for starting the end so close to the sideline that he may be blocked on his way down, or rendered useless on a kick into the opposite corner of the field. He should start at least ten yards from the sideline. There is no means of knowing precisely where the greatest strength will be needed down the field, and therefore it should be distributed as equally as possible on both sides of the ball. The ball should be kicked to the weakest back, if there is a known weakness. But otherwise it should be kicked down the center of the field. That gives the team its best chance to bring collective ability to bear in preventing the runback. To avoid kicking to strength, kick to the left-hand corner if possible. The two best tacklers should be so placed in the line as to give them the shortest possible route to reach the probable receiver of the kick. As in going down under a punt, the chief word of advice here is speed, speed, speed. It is far better to be blocked and thrown flat, while going fast, than to stand around the field dodging, without even the satisfaction of bumping the man who knocked you down. Every man going down should be specifically instructed to run straight to the receiver and to take a hard, smashing drive at him, miss or no miss. The receiver's interference is rendered useless to him if he is compelled to dodge tacklers instead of taking advantage of that interference.

The ends may be reminded that they are the guardians of the wings. A mistake that allows the runner to pass inside of them into the range of some one's else hard tackle is much less dangerous than the mistake which allows the runner to pass between the end and the sideline. If every man is coached, day after day, to follow these instructions, calling upon himself at every stride down the field to nm, nm, run, there will be no serious runback of any kick-off, in the present inadequate development of that play.

One accurate tackier should be left behind at midfield as a reserve against a possible failure to carry out these instructions, and also to save his team as much ground as possible in the event of a return kick; a play neglected in recent years, yet one of the most thrilling in football; and one of the best plays in the game, provided the opportunity is offered to a good, accurate kicker. As a rule, this man has plenty of time to make his return kick, with only one opponent to cover it. If he has any ability whatever in placing a kick, he can at once put his team out of danger. In a large majority of cases he needs no assistance, and has plenty of time to make his kick from his own fifteen-yard line. His single opponent is generally standing at the center of the field, especially if the return is not expected. A reasonable kick in distance and direction should roll well down into the enemy's territory, with delightful possibilities in the way of a recovered fumble.

Wonderful opportunities are open theoretically to the team receiving the kick-off. But the required skill, cooperation and finesse necessary to their realization cannot be acquired except by intensive practice of a most exhausting kind. This to the exclusion of drill in other important requirements. During the course of the short football season no other department of play is more neglected than the initial play of a contest. Successful coups on the kick-off keep some coaches awake and bring dreams to others. But in actual practice coaches soon become lukewarm, realizing that the players cannot, or will not, specialize with enthusiasm, or even fulfil ordinary kick-off assignments, unless strong pressure is brought to bear. The kaleidoscopic appearance of the broken field seems to exert a species of mesmerism on most players, and they fail to act. On the kick-off there is a great deal of running about and a general air of excitement, but it is very seldom that more than one man of the team coming down the field is checked so hard that he is actually thrown. Players who become thoroughly accustomed to ordinary scrimmage conditions, so that they feel entire self-possession and accustomedness in the heart of the battle, seldom outgrow the sensation of bizarre strangeness which the kick-off produces. It is evocative of all the nervous strain and stage fright which can be associated with one's first moment of participation in a regular game. The amount of lost effort and wasted motion indulged in by the players receiving a kick-off can only be matched by similarly misdirected effort of the equally rattled battalions who come charging down the field. Yet this play, the despair of coaches, infinite in its possibilities, is bound to be mastered in time by some combination of team, temperament and ability which will really undertake with seriousness to make something out of the kick-off; instead of being content, as most teams are, to get a runback by dint of reasonable effort and individual skill which shall be at least equivalent to a touchback.

I am convinced that it would be worth a coach's while to have laid out a miniature gridiron somewhere on his athletic field, where kick-off plays could be demonstrated and practiced by walking through them. Then the loss of time and the excessive fatigue involved in drill on the making and receiving of kick-offs could be avoided. The blackboard, also, is an instrument whereby a great deal of valuable instruction can be given to a team which has really made up its mind collectively to develop the extraordinary possibilities of open field play. Nearly everything that can be imagined in connection with the kick-off has, of course, been attempted, at one time or another. The trouble is that these attempts have seldom, if ever, been carried out with the necessary faith, enthusiasm determination and careful devotion to detail which players and coaches willingly expend on other matters.

The two chief reasons why most planning for the runback of kick-offs comes to naught are, first, the individual's failure to pick out definitely the man to be blocked; second, the failure of him who does pick a man to stay on one side or the other of this individual. Instead, the blocker inveterately places himself directly in front of his charging opponent, who is thus enabled to force the blocker to two guesses as to the direction in which he will dodge. It should be a long step toward the working out of really brilliant kick-off plays when blockers universally accept the idea that the way to function surely is to stay on one side of the man to be blocked, and force him to go to the other side. The blocker must then be alert, ready to spring, and all as convincing in his final lunge as if he were a tackier and his opponent a runner with the ball. As a matter of common experience, this degree of sincerity can seldom be found at the kick-oft except where the blocker has the incentive of knowing that the actual runner with the ball is directly behind him, and must be protected.

The players are seldom altogether to blame for their Laodicean mental attitude. It is very infrequently the case that there are many specific arrangements to guide forward blockers. The receiver, whether he has a plan or not, is exceedingly likely to run where he sees opportunity. Most coaches are content that he should do so, if he is a speedy and capable man. But when the receiver does throw a prearranged plan to the winds, it means simply that the blocker cannot be certain whether he is driving his man into the runner or away from him. The resulting decline in his sincerity of effort is at least pardonable. There are many sensational plays in which an ideal team receiving the kick-off might be as well instructed as is the ordinary team in its everyday working offense. There are also a few simple combinations with which even an ordinary team may experiment profitably.

There is, for example, the run by an outside back, eventually down the sideline, but not until he has made a feint toward the center. Here the runner starts in the direction that the blockers intend to charge their opponents. As the feint is made toward the center, the blockers place themselves outside their respective victims, thus allowing them the path they now desire. Then, at the proper moment, the blockers charge their men, dropping them if they can; at least driving them still farther toward the center of the field. The runner with the ball turns toward the sideline at the same moment. The players assigned to interfere for him, knowing his eventual course, place themselves where they can aid him if he does reach the sideline.

Another plan with an everyday working possibility of success is to put all the strength possible on the two outside men of the kicking team, on one side of the field or the other, according to the direction of the run; sending the runner, with whatever interference can be given him, straight up the field. This plan presupposes a kick to either corner.

As for the often-practiced general retreat of the receivers to a point where they can form a solid wall, or wedge, for the runner's protection, it can only be said that this maneuver usually results in the entanglement of the runner in such a maze of arms, legs and bodies that he cannot make any progress. It is a mere confusion of twenty-one men, and a hopeless task. The cloud of interferers may serve somewhat to mask a well-ordered crisscross play. But even then there must be a very careful organization of forces for the taking out of converging tackles on the side where the ultimate runner is intended to emerge. The crisscross, unfortunately, only serves, as a rule, to bring kicking-side players into effective action who would otherwise find themselves unable to participate in the play.

For any team which has no definite program for the receiving of kick-offs, and for all teams on short or on low, fast kicks, a straight run up the field is always the best move. The runner at least obtains some positive result, measurable in yards; whereas a detour seldom succeeds. Moreover, the runner who goes straight will encounter the fewest possible number of men who must be dodged.

Most teams, as I have said, are satisfied if they are reasonably confident, in a hazy sort of way, that they can at least run kick-offs back to the twenty- or twenty-five-yard line, and that their opponents can do no better, But the team which could be equally certain, and with a better show of reason, that it could reach the thirty-five yard mark with any kick-off which did not go deep into touch, would be a very hard team to beat, other things being anywhere near equal. Coaches should know after hearing reports on the personnel of opponents in two or three games, where the likeliest path lies for a runback, in case the receiver has the power of selection. If possible, also, the coach should carefully diagram the opponents' lineup for the kick-off and indicate and identify the men to be blocked. But few coaches actually go much further than to develop blocking by their center, guards and tackle as far as possible, counting on their ends and backs to interfere as well as to block. They do this usually without giving specific assignments, as the players on the kick-off are so far apart that there is little likelihood of several blockers picking the same man. They merely enforce the general rule that the fastest man is the man to take out.

A word as to the position of receivers on the kick-off: it is quite unnecessary to stand the ends, tackles and outside backs so close to the sidelines as the usual arrangement does. The backs, moreover, commonly play too deep. The center should stand twelve yards from the ball, and be instructed to let it alone if it comes fast to him. If he attempts to handle it he may fumble, with the odds tremendously against recovery. He should handle all "topped drives," however, and slow-rollers generally.

The two guards should play some three yards deeper than the center, thirty yards apart and equidistant from their respective sidelines. The tackles should station themselves at the twenty-five-yard line, the quarter at the twenty, the ends eighteen yards from the goal line and the three backs at the ten-yard mark. These positions are interchangeable, in the sense that the best men running with the ball should play the deepest. The quarter and the fullback should be centered with respect to the goals. The tackles and outside backs, or those substituted for them, should stand ten yards from the sideline, and the ends fifteen yards from the borders of the field.

This arrangement gives a much more closely united formation than is generally seen, and the problem of becoming effective is simplified thereby. Any kick that is likely to go out of bounds can be covered, if it seems to be good judgment to cover it; while on long kicks the backs have ample time in which to retreat. Usually it is very unwise to attempt a runback if the kick goes into touch; and at best it is a rash procedure.

The kick-off is a somewhat dangerous play, as plays go, from the standpoint of safety from injury; but the danger would be largely eliminated if the players executed their assignments with the proper degree of enthusiasm. The universal use of headgear, and determined effort with muscles properly expanded, would eliminate finally whatever special danger may be said to exist.

CHAPTER XXXIII: ONSIDE KICK AND PUNT-OUT

The onside, or quarterback, kick decidedly deserves to be included in the repertoire of a first-class team. It is a play of tremendous possibilities, with many incidental advantages accruing even when it is not successful in its main object. Not even the long forward pass gives opponents a more acute mental shock. The ball should be kicked flat, as in the case of a punt-out, with the long axis held at right angles to the kicking foot instead of in a line with the latter. A backfield jump shift to the right preferably precedes the kick, which should be directed high enough to go over the defensive halfback's head if sent to the wide side of the field; or it may be kicked thirty-five or forty feet in the air, giving the outside backs time to get under it. Being onside they are entitled to catch the ball, even though in so doing they interfere with a catch by an opponent. They need not look up for the kick until the last moment, as the defensive halfback will indicate the spot to them. Success depends on their speed.

The ends and the left tackle, although not on side, are going down the field. They should look up and locate the ball, to cover it in case the kick is fumbled by an onside player of either team. The remainder of the line, together with the kicker, also get the direction of the ball as soon as they hear the sound of the kick and cover the danger zone to prevent a possible runback.

Figure the possibilities for yourself. In case the ball strikes the ground, you have six players of the kicking side against one of the opponents, with the defensive fullback coming up late. Viewed from any angle, this play, properly worked, gives more than fifty per cent of the chances to the kicking team, if the backfield is reasonably agile. If the ball is recovered by the kicker's side, a touchdown is imminent. Anywhere between your own forty and your opponents' thirty-yard line, the onside kick is a standard play.

Warning is elsewhere given against heeling a fair catch so as to prevent the catcher from taking even the two additional steps which the law allows. This applies especially to receivers of the punt-out; concerning which play a few suggestions occur. The team making a punt-out has ten men left. Four of them should cover the field; or this number may be reduced to three, if the kicker is especially accurate. The remainder should line up as near to the goal line as the rules allow; because the sooner block-ing starts, the less the speed of the players scored upon, and the more effective the blocking.

This line-up should not be a scattering of players indiscrimi-nately. If the kick is decently directed it will fall at a point some-where in front of the goal. At any rate, so the scored-on team supposes, and it makes its charge there. The blockers should so line up as to cover approximately the width of the goal. They should not charge. Three of them would be likely, if they did, to pick the same charger. They should await the advance, each blocking the most natural man. The special punt used for this play should be practiced often. The ball is kicked flat on the instep, and dropped with its length parallel to the body, instead of at a right-angle as in punting generally. This is a very simple kick, and for short distances can be very accurately delivered.

The method of holding the ball for a try-at-goal after a touch-down or punt-out is as follows:

The holder of the ball having placed himself on the side of the kicker's leg, preferably lies on his stomach and elbows. This position gives him absolute ease and steadiness, the knuckles of the left hand touching the ground, the lower end of the ball resting on the forefinger and middle finger spread, the end of the ball protruding slightly below the fingertips, the upper end of the ball controlled by the forefinger and middle finger of the upper hand. It may be necessary to raise the right elbow from the ground, depending on the length of the holder's forearm. Now as the holder moves the ball to place it on the ground the fingers do not interfere in any way and have no tendency to tilt the ball when they are withdrawn. This is the most important feature. The pressure by the fingers of the right hand is only sufficient to steady the ball.

Zealous referees often annoy the kicker considerably on this play. In their anxiety that no advantage shall be given the kicking team they frequently place themselves too close to the ball. They could as readily see the ball placed and signal the defenders as promptly from a convenient distance. At the request of the kicker the referee will be very willing to retire to a position equally as good.

CHAPTER XXXIV: GENERALSHIP VS. ZONE PLAY

As in most modem affairs, there is a marked tendency in our football to over-systematize. I refer particularly to zone play. Zone play, as is well known, calls for certain specific strategic moves when a team has the ball near its own goal line; for another set of hard and fast rules when the ball has been secured toward the center of the field, or as its progress is toward either sideline, and for almost equally conventional tactics within the forty-yard-line of the opponents.

This perpetual, more or less logical, shifting of attack and defense, according to position in the different zones of the playing field, has been so well advertised and taught by football writers and coaches that its importance and necessity have assumed the purple of accepted fact. But its actual value is all the more debatable for that very reason.

Zone play is perpetuated very largely because of the natural unwillingness of coaches to bring down upon their own heads a storm of adverse criticism, seriously weakening their prestige, by adopting unconventional tactics which might not operate successfully. A football coach occupies a very difficult position. He often wishes to try plays that he knows instinctively would baffle the defending team, but his aversion for injurious criticism, as well as his fear that his judgment and knowledge may be questioned, deters him. It is to be regretted that a successful forward pass from the throwers' five-yard line would be heralded as a fine bit of deception, while the same play, meeting with failure, would be everlastingly held up as proof of a coach's utter lack of sense or judgment. Such a criticism as this the astute coach must hope to avoid.

The inevitable result of his consequent self-repression is a style of play in the attacking team's own territory so conservative as to allow an experienced player on defense to predict almost without failure what the opposing quarterback will elect to do. Of course, this robs the game of much of its natural dash, ingenuity and thrill. It impregnates football with two much of that rather undesirable quality of conservatism. There is no reason why the game should be injured, or a competent coach attacked, because he dares to attempt more than his rivals.

Better football would be seen if players could be taught to feel that the presence near the goal line of opponents with the ball is particular cause not for despair but rather for thrills, offering opportunity to do something really big. I venture to say that the team which disregarded adverse criticism and constantly attempted the "desperate chances" throughout the season, even though failure should result now and then, would show the greatest comparative degree of improvement at the end of the season, and the finest spirit on defense as well as on attack.

Some of the biggest games in late years have been lost by the withholding of a particularly strong running attack, or of a particularly strong runner from the team, until the auspicious moment is expected to arrive when the team shall be within striking distance of the enemy's goal line. The time to score is in the first minute of the game, if possible; if not then, in the next minute. The earlier the lead, the surer the victory and the brighter the bonfire. Why should abundant dash, strength and virility be saved for a final crash? It is a poor player whose strength does not increase as he lessens the distance between himself and a touchdown.

Not so very many years ago a football game consisted of two forty-five-minute halves, undivided into periods with breathing space between. Substitutions were infrequent, and the player leaving the game might not return. Men were kept in until practically exhausted. The game itself was fully as rugged as it is today. Possession of the ball was considered four-fifths of the game. Kicking as a means of offense was considered only in connection with a strongly favoring wind, and by many of the best teams not even then. The backs involved had no more stamina than ours. Yet they rushed into their line-smashing, head-crashing plays and their foot-crushing revolving wedges without a thought of physical collapse or fast-approaching senility; and considered it a great disgrace to be removed from the game. Yet we moderns are perpetually worrying lest we waste too suddenly our halfbacks' physical power in a short game of an hour; with two resting spells between periods and fifteen minutes between the halves; with considerably fewer than half the actual number of plays; with considerably less physical exertion per play; with a great cloud of substitutes, most of whom get into the game; with the right of re-substitution, so that players bathed, rubbed, warmed, fed, newly equipped and rested for a half hour or more, are able to return to the game.

Send your quarterbacks into the game untrammeled by the superstition of zone play, and start the game with your strongest lineup under the conditions. Zone play is an invention of coaches based on excessive, however excusable, conservatism and their distrust of their field general's good sense. Unquestionably, from the standpoint of danger, the offensive team near its own goal line is by far in the more nervous condition after the first kick-off. This applies to teams of all classes, and a touchdown by opponents caused by a bad fumble in the early moments of the game would have a most depressing effect. With this exception, quarterbacks should be encouraged to use their offense and not to withhold it; kicking before a strong wind or by a highly superior kicker naturally grouping itself under the head of offense. Zone play practically amounts to this: coaches who would like to instruct the quarter before every play, and may not, instruct him instead for a series of plays. These plays are so conservative that nothing short of a fumble can resolve the situation. Unless you kill the zone play idea in your quarterback you are perpetually reminding him of the possibility of a fumble. Is this wise?

Let us put two teams on the field. One has kicked off, the other has made a reasonable runback, and is somewhere near the twenty-yard line. According to the tactics laid down for a team which is presumably using zone play, and eliminating the wind altogether, there is now but one thing to do — kick the ball. The fullback retires to about the ten-yard line. The game has just started. Both teams are nervous. The kicking team is by far in the more dangerous position, and consequently much the more nervous of the two.

The more nervous team now elects to do a much more dangerous thing than running with the ball. The center must make a long and, at this stage of the game, an exceedingly dangerous pass. If his nerve is good, he may send the ball over the kicker's head. If his nerve is doubtful, probably he will make a low pass, which the kicker cannot convert into a successful punt without serious liability to blocking. Even though the pass be excellent, there is still danger from blocking, and no little likelihood of a poor punt. In cold blood, does punting appear to be good judgment?

Let us say that the best which may be hoped for happens. The ball is punted, the kick is covered, and it is first down for the receiving team at the middle of the field; a very good boot, and no runback. The receiving team, which is also an exponent of zone play, probably will make two attempts to carry the ball, at least one of them at tackle, and, if unsuccessful, will punt. Many teams, however, I am glad to say, will either set forth on the path to a touchdown, or punt on the first down.

By all means at this time the very best men are in both lineups. If there was ever a time when they are needed it is in the early part of the game, when not even veterans are proof against nerve shock. The ball is punted to the fifteen-yard line, the receiver catches and is nailed with a slight gain. It is now up to the team in possession to punt again, with the kicker stranding somewhere in the vicinity of his five-yard line. He faces all the difficulties that beset him before, with perhaps slightly less nervousness. With a reasonable break he cannot hope to get better than the middle of the field again, where the ball goes once more to the opponents.

Looking at the game from any fair angle, with both teams evenly balanced and both teams handling punts cleanly, these exchanges might reasonably be kept up throughout the period; with the great mental burden on the team which is backed up against its own goal line. If a break does occur, it is reasonably certain that this team will be the sufferer by it. Therefore, nothing could have justified this team in continuing to kick except pronounced superiority in the kicking game. Under ordinary circumstances, the team playing its big rival knows its superiority or inferiority in the kicking game before it goes on the field. Surely, then, if the teams are balanced in kicking, or if the team receiving the kick-off is inferior in this respect, zone play has no justification whatever. It is very easy to see, then, that without a favoring wind, or a much better kicker and ability to cover, the less favored team must depend upon luck, or find some other means of getting out of its dilemma.

The only justification for even the first punt is the nervousness apparent at the beginning of the game. Even then, and because of this very nervousness, it would be better to try one running play, with the surest back to carry the ball. Even if this play is unsuccessful, and probably it will be, the first wild moment of panic is at an end, and the team is in much better condition to kick.

On the other hand, should a substantial gain be made, even of three or four yards, we are justified in considering the probable result of a kick. We know that in a few minutes or less we shall have the same problem on our hands again. The team has cooled down and is steady. It has been somewhat surprised and very much pleased by the result of its first attack. You have told your team that they are a crowd of fighters, and they believe it. Why not attempt to end the everlasting defense of the goal line before it begins? If this can be accomplished, even the hardened advocates of zone play will cheer for you.

I do not wish to make myself an advocate of senseless, indiscriminate offense as the means of getting out of a difficult situation. The quarterback should not resort to a hap-hazard pounding of the line at this or any other time.

The football coach should plan each play, with almost no exceptions, so that, perfectly executed, it should score. But there are certain plays which have greater probabilities than others. The quarterback should have full authority to use any play in his list, if warranted in so doing by any modification in the defense. Zone players play zone play on the defense as well as on the attack. They assume zone play by the attacking team, and are accustomed to act accordingly. The quarterback, watchful of defensive readjustment, should take any possible advantage of it.

For example, zone players against a team struggling in this part of the field will immediately assume a preponderance of tackle or end plays, trick plays, perhaps, but no forward passes. What then is more strategic than plays inside a wide-playing tackle, or a forward pass in which the risk of interception is negligible?

All competent coaches would attempt these things but for the fear of ruinous adverse criticism. One of the big varsity teams of the east so invariably assumes its opponents are slaves to zone play that year after year it crowds its secondary defense within six yards of the line for two downs, in the firm conviction that no forward pass will be dared by a team in its own half of the field. This university has suffered defeats by scores by no means indicative of its very genuine excellence in many departments of football. Against a team so playing its secondary defense, it is a very simple matter to throw deep forward passes from running attack formations without the slightest possibility of interception. Against any team there are various long forward passes not always recoverable by one's own ends but always safe from interception by opponents.

Returning now to our theoretical team which has received its kick-off, lined up at the twenty-yard mark, tried one play to steady itself and gained some four yards. Its quarterback has decided to make an immediate attempt to put his own goal line well behind him, instead of attempting to defend it for perhaps a full period. Assuming normal positions by the defense, his best attack, in my opinion, would be as follows: inasmuch as the defense is set, fresh and determined to stop the only kind of attack outside of a kick that it expects as probable, I would attempt first the long, safe forward pass. The defensive fullback, who is especially sensitive to the probability of a kick under these conditions, is playing deep. The attempt, whether successful or not, is a big shock to the defensive team. I will not admit that, properly-planned, it is of special danger to the offensive team. If it is successful it means a very substantial gain, probably well into opponents' territory. If unsuccessful, the next best play from the standpoint of danger to the offensive team is a simple, carefully executed trick play, while the defense is in a slightly perturbed frame of mind, probably expecting another forward pass so that its secondary defense is slightly drawn back. If this play is successful, conditions have altered greatly to the advantage of the team carrying the ball. If unsuccessful, the last possible play that the defense can expect will be a straight attack. The quarterback should size up quickly, without giving special evidence of so doing, the positions of the defensive linemen. After two such plays, and in the thorough expectation now of either a punt or a wild, long-distance effort, the line probably will be well spread. If so, I would make a strong attempt inside of tackle. But if the defensive line is normally spaced I would try to carry the ball outside of tackle.

"But," comes the possible objection, "it is now fourth down, and you must punt. Therefore the defensive team will make a particularly wholehearted effort to block the kick." Is there likely to be any effort here to block the kick that would not have been present had the kick been attempted on the first down? My answer would be no. But the team has had three opportunities to alter the aspect of the game in its favor. Had it succeeded on any of the three, the necessity of a continual goal line defense would have been averted; and this was the necessity we expended our energies to dispel. Next it is objected that we are expending the rushing power of our team in a part of the field where it does no good; taking, furthermore, the chances of a fumble which easily might spell disaster. So far as the fumble is concerned, what is the difference between a fumble here, with slight chance that the adversary could run away with the ball if he got it, and the fumble of the everlasting kick that he will everlastingly force us to handle at the fifteen-yard mark? That fumble, if it occurs, will be received by him, beyond any reasonable doubt, and very possibly for a touchdown. The greater danger lies in the latter.

As for the exhaustion of the team in running attack, what has been done so far to produce excessive fatigue? There have been exactly four plays. We have heard so much talk, and read so much criticism, on the subject of zone play, which claims for its principle in this part of the field the conservation of energy, that our cool judgment and common sense have been stifled. One might suppose our football team composed of eleven anemic cripples.

Another objection: "You have now only one down in which to kick." The answer is that no team needs more, unless it has reason to suspect its own kicking game; and in this discussion we are assuming competent teams at the height of their season. I have seen high-grade teams attempt a field goal on the second down. I would look upon such an attempt favorably if attempted from the forty-five-yard line. It would have the effect of a punt at worst, and if successful would be a heartbreaker for the opponents. But as the attempt was made from the thirty-five-yard line, it gave the impression that the team was saving downs against possible poor passes or fumbles; and such a reckless waste of opportunity is a great breeder of timidity. There is a possible fumble in every play.

At any rate, we are now going to punt, on the fourth down; although there are a number of things which I would rather do. Here is undoubtedly sound cause for a kick. The average man expects it. In three downs you have failed to gain your distance. Unquestionably good judgment calls for a kick. But that judgment is based on conservatism. We punt accordingly; though sound judgment is robbing us of our very best opportunity. There is not a man on the opposing team who would not wager his quarter's allowance that the play is to be a punt, and we do not disappoint him, for even Achilles was not brave every day.

But for the sake of illustrating further the operations of attack in different parts of the field, let us assume that each of our three attempts succeeded in varying degrees. Let us take first our tackle play, which carried the ball to the forty-yard line, let us say.

We should now have two guiding thoughts: First, if we are forced to kick, through inability to advance the ball otherwise, we are relieved from the strain of working under the shadow of our goal posts; and this displeases our opponents as much as it pleases us. Second, teams which are strongly inclined to the habit of zone play, whether they call it by that or by some other name, expect that, under the present conditions, with the ball on our own forty-yard line, we will try two running plays; and, if not successful, we will punt on the third down. If the two plays are fairly successful, almost accomplishing a first down, and we line up in kick formation, the only other serious fear they will have is the bare possibility of a forward pass from this formation. But the thought of their opponent attempting a forward pass on either the first or second down they would not dream of entertaining. Therefore we have the key to the most logical possible play for either the first or second down, namely a forward pass. But on the previous first down we tried a forward pass. And we must assume that our opponents are bright enough to take the tip. Our team is bold and rash enough to violate the laws of the Medes and Persians! The forward pass is therefore the play they now are more than half inclined to expect. So instead we will take a crack at the other tackle; or try the same tackle hole again with a different play. In either case our gain is small. But we have gleaned a little information.

Now, says the quarterback, we will try a forward pass. We want to make particularly sure that it will not be intercepted. Let us try the one we failed with before, but pass the ball to another eligible man. The quarterback is about to give his signal when his rapid survey of the defensive lineup apprises him of the fact that the defensive fullback has doped out another long forward pass as the probable play. Having been caught too deep in the backfield on the previous occasion, the fullback has now stationed himself some twenty yards from the line of scrimmage. Immediately, through thorough coaching, the quarterback sees that a quick kick from regular formation undoubtedly will sail over the fullback's head. There is no indication from the offensive formation that a kick is threatened.

The signal is given, the ball is snapped and the first indication of danger is when the defensive fullback hears the thud of a halfback's foot against the ball. In consternation he sees that he has fallen into a trap, and that the ball is sailing far over his head into the sacred regions that he was supposed to guard.

A kick that goes over the fullback's head and does not go into touch is a very long kick. A mediocre kick, if allowed to roll, will go fifty yards. This particular kick is made from as good a spot as any to go far enough and not too far. Now let the zone playing team, with the shoe on the other foot, attempt by zone tactics to get themselves out of difficulty. Our team has played six plays, and, under assumptions that are not unreasonable, the ball is now in possession of the team kicking off, far down near its own goal line.

But let us suppose that we reached the middle of the field on our trick play, in the first series of downs. The quarterback who takes his team for first down on the fifty-yard line should remember two things. He can at any time without adverse criticism call for a punt; for the punter will be but sixty yards from the adversary's goal line. If his team is able to prevent a runback, it will place opponents in the same unenviable situation which the so-far successful team occupied at the beginning of the game. A kick even on the first down would be good football. On the other hand, a perfectly good quarterback would be showing sound judgment in attempting a march for a touchdown right here.

"But," urge objectors, "why continue to reveal the character of your offense at this time, giving opponents such full opportunity to study and diagnose it that in the second half they will be able to meet your plays with perfected defense?" This objection will surely be offered. I am entirely out of patience with such reasoning. If the ball happened to be on opponents' forty- instead of fifty-yard-line, the same objectors would throw off the quarterbacks' harassing instructions and give the command: "Now hit them with everything you have for a touchdown." Admittedly it may be more difficult to cover fifty yards than forty; but why throw away opportunity? Logically, zone play advocates should recommend a kick on first down when at midfield. They weaken their argument by essaying any plays whatever, as they do, before kicking.

Regarding the supposition that diagnosis and special coaching between halves can kill an offense, it may be true if the coaches, whoever they are, can supply their team with the determination it lacked in the first half. The team that has failed thus far has known for the past week, at least, the general style of its opponents' offense, and a very large majority of the plays that will be met. It has received the best instruction available to defend against them. Instruction given during intermission may be very useful. But the intermission is hardly long enough to embrace a discussion of an entire system of offense.

Diagnosis, as a matter of fact, is as necessary for the attacking as for the defensive team. A team may try a play half a dozen times before it discovers the diagnosis of the other team, to the extent of taking full advantage of it. On a tackle play one must know the defense of the tackle and end not only, but of the guard and defensive quarter as well, before specifying to an exact degree the one best point to puncture the line on that play. Furthermore, the particular action of the guard, as well as the defensive quarterback, gives a complete key to the weakness of the guard position if we run a play through guard from this same formation; a delayed buck, for example.

The quarterback must have information as to the habits of the defensive line and its methods of defense before he can pick his plays with certain knowledge. The sooner that a team can start its offense, within reason, the sooner it will know the defense it must break down. "Holding back attack for the second half" means that you do not know enough about the defense to take advantage of its weaknesses when you do cut loose.

"Does this apply to the trick play?" Have we then only one? How many teams ever used in their final game all the plays they had? You've always some more stuff, and the time to use any play is the time when one is satisfied that the play will work.

Now let us take the third case and suppose that our long forward pass, thrown so unconventionally early in the game, was recovered. On this pass, if entirely successful, the runner can only be stopped by the defensive fullback. If the end is a good runner, the fullback has less than an even chance to get him. But suppose that the runner is pulled down at opponents' twenty-yard-line. The one big thing we are up against now is that we have had no opportunity to try out the defense of our opponents by running attack. Therefore in the selection of plays our quarter-back can have but three important guides: first, his best ground-gainers throughout the season; second, any apparent defects in the positions assumed by individual defenders; third, information through scouting concerning individual weakness in defense. His supreme thought, until conditions make it impossible, is a touch-down. His teammates to a man must know that this thought fires his heart, soul and body. Every man on the team is inspired by the same desire, including the drop-kicker or placekicker if you have one. It is a tense moment for the good captain. He knows very well what he considers now to be the best play. He knows even better that this is the time above all times that he should keep off. He must do nothing to break the unanimity of thought and action.

The best this quarterback can now do is to take it easy; show confidence in his teammates; speak words of assurance to them; call out the word, "Signal," in order to get the defensive players set as nearly as possible in their defensive positions; digest what-ever information he can thus obtain; consider the information that he had already regarding individuals in the opposing line, and adapt the total to his strongest play. He must avoid above all things at this stage a forward pass of such length that, if not covered, it would result in a touchback. Every quarterback should know this, but I have seen the error committed often. He should play at least two of his best plays, in my opinion three; and then take in his situation as to his next move. Of course, unless he has received specific instructions to the contrary, his final move will depend upon the success or failure of the three plays attempted. If it is reasonably possible to make first down on the fourth play, the attempt should be made. A forward pass on the fourth down is expected by the opponent, unless a position is assumed by the attacking team to try a field goal. The coach must have his quarterback instructed carefully in generalship under these very conditions. There must be a decision here whether the ball shall be rushed, with a good chance to rush it, or whether a special scoring play shall be attempted. Many ifs, ands and buts crowd themselves upon the quarterback's mind.

In case the chance for a first down is hazardous, the decision must be made between a stroke for a touchdown and an attempt at a field goal. The efficiency of your drop-kicker is one of the factors to be considered. The field goal opportunity should not be passed up unless the quarterback has an especially deceptive trick play or forward pass which the coach has given him with special instructions for its use at just such a time. At this stage of the game, any score puts the team scoring in the lead. If the field goal is particularly sure, it is a hard thing to pass up. If it seems slightly surer than the scoring play, take the field goal. If the chances are about even, take the big scoring play.

CHAPTER XXXV: "H HOUR"

The preliminary schedule of games should provide plenty of first-class competition, and nothing less than that accords with the proper and high ideals of the game. It is a great mistake, however, for a coach to arouse and excite the players before every contest. He may happen to possess genuine ability as an orator and spell-binder, but decidedly he should reserve his efforts for the greater occasions, urging his men for the present only in accordance with the importance of the game.

He should lay special emphasis on the features of the practice during the week, the new plays acquired and their practical application in the forthcoming contest. In very concise, unemotional language he should recite, first to the players according to their positions and finally to the team, the dos and don'ts which he desires to make a part of their second nature. If this is done before every game he can make the lesson so familiar that before the final game he can review it practically in pantomime, and very quickly, before turning loose the flood of his final appeal. I append an outline of what I usually say in the dressing room in the way of general instruction. It runs substantially as follows:

Centers: Remember that you are masters of the ball — whether you are in possession or not, be the first to get to the ball when a down is declared. You are the guardians of the ball. Take care of it, within the rules, whether on attack or defense. When you pass, send it through with confidence and get away to the charge. Your backs will take care of the ball. In your enthusiasm to charge, don't raise the ball and leave it in the air, in the belief that you have passed it. A fumble by the quarter usually means the center's failure to complete his pass. It is perfectly simple to make the pass and to charge simultaneously. When passing for a kick, remember that it is just as easy as it was in scrimmage against the second team. Be sure of your preparations, and then give the pass no further thought. Send it back hard. We'll get it. Don't roll it on the ground.

"Guardians of the Ball"
Harris & Ewing

Guards: You have a great opportunity. Don't be picture guards. You have the best opportunities to block kicks. You have as good a chance as anybody to go down under punts and tackle the runner. Guard on the short side of an unbalanced line, besides your other duties remember that you charge through to get the quarterback on his runs at center. You have another special task, to watch the center for information. Watch the position of his hands in passing. If you see a change, warn your team as you have been instructed.

Tackles: You must bear the brunt of the defense. The number of runners with the ball you take down is of no account. On close formation charge through end, with head, shoulders and arms. Go behind the enemy's line of scrimmage. Don't play defensive on the other side of the line by chasing plays. You are not a diagnostician, you are primarily a wrecker of plays at or near you. Charge through your side of the line when sure the play is going the other side. After you have done this, then chase the play and try to figure in it. It means more wear and tear to your opponents when they lack the determination to fight you off which they would have were they trying to build a hole through you. Furthermore, you are likely to meet a check play on your way through. Tackles on kick formations, I want you to do two things going down under kicks. Here they are in order of importance: charge the defensive guard hard; tackle the receiver of the punt. You may not aspire to All-American tackle by getting under kicks fast and tackling accurately down the field if in doing so you have allowed your guard free path to block the kick; because you won't be on the team.

Ends: I am looking for you today to do well two jobs. On offensive, beat down the tackle. I must have this, or you can't play end. Remember your great aid; to worry him by continual shifting of position when the play is going to the other side of the line. Then get him right, when you need it. Early in the game, try this defensive tackle out. See how far he'll go out with you. If he's generous, take advantage of it later. This perpetual shifting will make it easier to go down under forward passes and kicks. When on the defensive, your great job is to camp in the opponents' backfield. Break through their plays before they are formed, Play slightly closer when the strength is on your side. Don't worry about your opponents gaining ground when their formation is on your side; worry about it when that formation is on the other side. When you charge into the backfield then, watch the scrimmage line and quarterback on your immediate side. Be ready for fakes, checks and crisscrosses. Always hurry the forward pass.

Never mind about the passes over your head. Some one else will care for them. Going down under kicks, remember your whole line is with you. Without any wide detour, force the receiver inside. Remember the best way to dodge the defensive halfback is by speed. If you hesitate his work is partly done whether he takes you down or not.

Quarterback: We are depending upon your judgment. You pick your own plays, until you are positively wrong. Keep the team in hand. If the wind is bad, or you are close to your goal line, he cool, go slowly, give your next play plenty of thought. When you've made your choice, snap your team into the play fast and hard. Your passing is good enough so that your backs will take the ball as a matter of course and without worry. In playing defensive fullback, keep in balance with the teams, keep the play within reach on both sides. Never let a loose runner face you straight ahead coming down the field. Get him on one side. Then don't waste effort. A few yards now will make little difference. Your job is to stop a touchdown. Hit him hard and take him down. We have a strong wind today. It's blowing diagonally across. When it's with you, use it. In the second half it may be gone. It's the legalized twelfth man on the team. Don't force your kicker, if it can be helped, to kick close to the sideline toward which the wind is blowing. Watch for bad spacing in the defense. Keep your eye on the secondary. If the fullback is playing short, put one over his head. Use the plan of attack that has been outlined to you, but, above all, use your best judgment.

Backs: Work hardest when you are faking, but be natural. If you fake at the end, keep him busy. You've been shown and you know that you can break through the line if the enemy is not breaking through. Prove it. Wear yourselves out as quickly as possible. Then come out. The subs will take your place. If you don't work, they'll take your place anyway. They are improving, and they need the work. If you must look around, look around before the signal is given. Take it easy; your signals are simple. Don't get the habit of yelling: "Signal." At the last moment if you don't know the play, call out. Complete every assignment. Don't know you are down till you can't get up. On defense, keep your eyes on the quarterback if he's under center. You can then see the two ends. Halfback on the side away from the formation, you can't leave your position till the backfield is positively on its way and you are sure where the ends are. This doesn't mean loafing; you'll see it all in the small part of a second. Defending against kicks, get the end, on one side or the other, and take him down or make him run wide. Take it for granted his motto is speed.

Defensive quarterback: You are the main prop of the defensive line. You have one of the finest jobs in the world. You need lots of eyesight. You can pick the attack on the line from the fake, for a lot of the backs can't fake. Don't go too seriously till the quarter-back goes. Make them hesitate to stick their noses beyond the line. Hit them hard when they come through. It's a great job, and a man's job. Make the most of it.

Kickers: Remember the direction of the wind. If you are up against it on the sideline on fourth down, be sure to turn your ball in toward the center of the field. With the wind, spend your extra energy trying to get height. Against the wind, try to hold them down. Remember the direction of the wind is as important against it as with it. When time is taken out, talk your kicking game over with your captain and quarterback, now and then.

Team: I want you to remember especially one thing today as always. Hate and abhor the scrimmage line! It is a restraining mark. By the rules of the game you are held there until the ball is snapped. Get away from it as quickly as you can. Leave it behind you. It will never get you anything. I want to see this rushline, on defense, whether in opponents' territory or on its own one yard line, on the ground, charging as one man with the snap of the ball; head and shoulders set; muscles distended; eyes forward and alert; fighting to the play, ready with body and arms at all times to take down the runner or his interference. If you do this, they can't come through. I want to see the whole line down under kicks, every man prepared to make the tackle; but I want to see no selfish avoidance of the defensive line in order to accomplish this result. Watch the defensive center and guards. Perhaps you will kick off. Every man who loafs on this play will see the rest of the game from the sidelines. Get your positive, helpful information to the quarterback at the first good opportunity. The whole team is to charge as one man with the snap of the ball. Don't forget the scrimmage line.

Many coaches make mistakes of expression after a game has been played. To conceal disappointment by laughing and jesting with players is a mistake. To show bitterness toward players who have erred is also a mistake. A defeated team is entitled to respectful sympathy; best shown by an attitude of reserved depression. The team should feel and know that the coach is deeply disappointed. He should keep to himself within reasonable limits until such time as another period of association naturally begins. At that time it will be his task to put both praise and blame where they belong.

CHAPTER XXXVI: THE FINISHING TOUCHES

One of the most effective methods of finishing off and polishing a team's offense for its final game is shadow scrimmage. The coach should stand in front of his regular team, and behind the second team's line, raising his hands above his head to signify plays. The varsity team should go through its entire repertoire of plays at a slow trot. There should be no tackling, and only a mild resistance by the second team. Every first-string player, however, should execute his assignment on every play in the form he has decided to adopt.

The object of this drill is to make certain that a team has not become careless in the small but ever important details; to preserve that last factor that makes ground-gaining certain: thoroughness.

Shadow defense, moreover, gives players a chance to consider carefully the particular appearance of the opposing backfield in the various plays as they approach the line. It raises in the players' minds many useful ideas as to the precise manner in which certain plays may best be stopped or advanced. Thus the player acquires the valuable habit and experience of thinking about these things as the plays come to them in harmless form.

The rope is a physical drill which aids enormously in putting the finishing touches on a team when it is not wise to order very much scrimmage. Those ten-yard charges under the taut-held rope — five yards to the line and five beyond, turn again and go

— are tremendous builders of muscles and endurance. There is no telling how much rope drill a team in condition can stand, but the wisest rule is to stop the exercise when you see the good men slowing down. Remember that the shorter men have an advantage in this drill if charging side by side with taller fellows. Therefore the men should be assigned to groups according to height. Even then it will always be noticeable that the tall men are the first to weaken under the strain.

"Dartmouth Football Team"
H.H.H. Langill

Even if a coach intends to hold out certain players for supreme moments, he ought to start the game with his strength. Never give the other team an initial impression of weakness! The coach who holds out important men at any time is taking a gamble. I will admit that I have taken risks of this kind myself occasionally; but very seldom, and only after a careful calculation of the chances.

For instance, in one game, played under almost impossible conditions of snow, rain, hail and deep mud especially, I held out four of my best men for the entire third period, and sent them back, after nearly three-quarters of an hour of rest, warm and dry, in fresh uniforms and shoes. I believe that they saved my team from defeat; but I had gambled, all the same, that there would be no scoring in the third period.

In this game the conditions were exceedingly poor for any kind of football, but especially for forward passing or kicking. A kick of twenty-five yards beyond scrimmage was a fine punt. Both teams gave up attempting to catch the ball, which seldom would roll five yards. Often it would bury its nose in the mud and spin. This was a very exceptional game.

Usually the regular men are so much better than the subs that one should play them all the way. At the same time, a coach should never hesitate to put in a good substitute for a regular man who is not going well. One of the hardest lessons coaches and trainers must learn is to take any injured man out; especially if that man is a star. Yet the good substitute, uninjured and fresh, is the better man of the two.

Frequently the source of amazement to the coach and rejuvenation to the team is the substitute, especially the back; but this only because his work is more noticeable than a line player's. He comes into the game strong and determined, eagerly embracing the golden opportunity. Many a defeat has he turned into victory. It took me a long time to become convinced of this, even after I had seen it done; but to the young coach who has yet to make up his mind I offer prayerfully this motto: "Do it now."

I must admit I am not in favor of singing or instrumental music for football players on the day of a big game. And if the student bands outside must play, I would prefer that they confine themselves to martial airs. The making of music, or listening to it, does not create a warlike attitude. Calm, quiet, dispassionate discourse, or walking, is a better way to pass the tense hours before a big match, which real football players should regard at least with a certain degree of seriousness.

The mass-meeting is one of the most wonderful institutions of college life. It gives a thrill which many a man will be able to recall until his dying day. This should not, however, be coarsened or cheapened by too frequent repetition. One uproarious mass-meeting will do as much as anything or anybody can to put the finishing touches on a team. Do not have too many of them. Save their glorious inspiration for the supreme occasion.

The best kind of a speech before a big football t game is the one which contains not too many specific reminders, which might give the players a feeling that they are still unprepared. They ought to feel that at least they know as much football as their opponents, and probably more; that the game resolves itself to a proposition of extreme individual effort and team play. The final exhortation should arouse the team to intense feelings of brotherhood, fealty and self-sacrifice. Within due limitations of decency and fair play, build a supreme determination to win. For while there may be honor and glory in defeat, it is not to court those glories and honors that a team goes forth to battle.

Between the halves, as at all other times, the coach must remember that the men are human. They will stand for abuse if necessary; but you should show them first that the abuse is justified.

Try to remember that their spirit of elation or depression rivals your own. Therefore, for the best interests of all concerned, see that the men are as comfortable as possible, and that all necessary things in the way of physical repair are undertaken immediately and silently. Remember that the men are watching astutely every move of the coach, whom they consider, after all, their main reliance in adversity. His first duty is to correct, as dispassionately as circumstances will permit, the errors of play, of commission and of omission. His second duty is to improve both offense and defense if possible. He must avoid generalities at this time. He must be specific. Above all things, if he expects a response from his men, he must be logical. If he does not know what to say, silence is far better than hit-or-miss fault-finding. He is, in the minds of his men, superior to them in judgment; and he must live up to his role. If the team is carrying out his teachings as well as it can, if it is simply outplayed by a superior antagonist, he must be fair. He must never let the team catch him off his balance, and thus give the impression that he is at a loss how to improve the situation. If the coach is at his wit's end, it is far better judgment to take no chances by way of random suggestions. Rather he should evolve some scheme by which to hide his perplexity. He might, for instance, take in turn three or four of his more reliable men, off at one side but in plain view of the rest of the team, and hold secret conversation with them, urging that they pull the team together by their own physical and mental power; anything to make it appear to the team that the coach is not at the end of his tether, and that there is still hope. Having in some manner created the impression that help is at hand, and that better results must come, the coach should make his appeal, putting all his power of thought and feeling into the final words. If he is a real coach his team will go forth to the second half rejuvenated, encouraged and determined.

CHAPTER XXXVII: GETTING UNDER HIS SKIN

It is well for a coach to discover, if he can, the short cut to the best there is in every boy; the most compelling influence that can be brought to bear on a given member of the squad. The game itself is usually the tie between coach and player, but not always. Sympathetic appreciation of what may be a mere whim has won the heart of many a difficult chap, who later became a tower of strength to the team, thanks to some improvement in his mental attitude.

No doubt football instinct, so called, first discovers itself in most boys, who are destined later to become proficient, through the natural inclination of red-blooded youth for a rough and tumble pastime which contains at least the simulacrum of danger. All boys experience the natural love of danger, but there are those who feel that they are not brave enough to play, and these are forced to satisfy their instincts by looking on; until, in many cases, the appeal of the game overcomes timidity. In the meantime, however, they are not without their value to the cause of football, providing, as they do, that chorus of applause which arouses vanity and emulation as surely then as in later years.

Along with the competitive instinct, the cooperative and protective urge begins to manifest itself in our football stars of the future. The youngster, in fact, keeps discovering fresh incentives to learn the game and become proficient, and presently football spirit is evolved for manly boys to reverence and cultivate.

Football follows naturally and logically after the running, dodging and wrestling play of children. But there is no occasion for discouragement with reference to boys who grow up under excessive parental restraint like invalids or weaklings, or in isolated localities where sport is not known. There have been very fine football players who never saw a football until enrolled as students in some higher institution of learning.

I have never seen anybody to whom American football did not make a strong appeal if he or she had studied the game long enough to understand the basic features of play. A battle of wits and of brawn, football offers the finest combination to normal man for opportunity and for glorious achievement. Its picturesque and spectacular elements and its setting are highly attractive to artistic temperaments and romantic spirits. Moreover, the fall of the year is the harvest time of more than the fruits of the field. It is the time, in temperate climates, when man turns from his more languid summer mood, seeking and desiring strenuous competition. The greatest sense of physical achievement is possible at this time of the year. And there is a glamour of romance in football that touches the heart of any young man who has ever had the blessing to get close enough to the game to arouse his interest.

And young men not only! While I was coaching the Denver Athletic Club team, I once sat at dinner with an expert accountant, and with a noted builder of railroads, whose guests we were. The accountant, whose acquaintance I was then making, took occasion almost immediately to remark that football did not appeal to him. He regarded it, he said, as a matter of brute strength entirely. As such, his attitude toward it was frankly contemptuous.

I ventured to challenge the position of my new acquaintance, observing that I had never found football to be a matter of physical strength alone, if only for the reason that I was never very strong myself; yet had played the game considerably, and was supposed, at least, to have been successful. "You, as an expert in accountancy," I remember saying, "should be interested in football: in our ability to move a man without touching him; in the mathematical calculations by which we arrive at our signals; in the often extraordinary sense of diagnosis shown by players of the defending team." I concluded my appeal by inviting my new acquaintance to visit the grounds of the Denver club, of which club he happened to be a member, in order to acquire a little first-hand knowledge of the game as a basis for better judgment.

"I'm always willing to be shown where I'm Wrong," was my fellow guest's answer, and as he, a successful man of sixty, had little to do during the afternoons, professionally, I was not surprised to see him oil the sidelines at the practice the very next day.

I had quite a bit of correcting and explaining to do, that afternoon, and, presently, on turning my head to locate a man who stood in special need of admonition, I was interested to note that my friend, the accountant, had poked his way into the midst of the squad, and that he was listening to me with an extremely flattering air of attention.

After the practice he approached me and said: "Mr. Cavanaugh: I am a little mite ashamed of myself. I never realized that there was so much thought involved in every play at football, or that you planned so much in every move of the attack. I'm afraid I'm long past the age to play football. I'm sixty. But would you mind if I attended practice here regularly? May I put on a suit and pick up what I can by mingling with the boys? I'll try not to be too much in the way." I said: "Delighted!"

He never missed an afternoon's practice all that autumn. I can remember, as if it were yesterday, crossing the cactus-covered fields to Colfax Park, and seeing always the shiny, bald head on the bleachers of one waiting to find out if we were ever going to come. My story of the expert accountant and the reformation of his attitude toward football shows how people often pass up things that would be the joy of their lives, if they would only try them.

There is something in the swoop and shock of a hard tackle at the knees which stirs a racial memory and satisfies an ancient desire; but the sense of tremendous things well done after making a perfect tackle is perhaps a more modem guerdon. After a perfect tackle, made in an instant, you realize that you are one hundred per cent perfect. That priceless thrill of exhilaration need not include the slightest sense of gloating over an opponent's overthrow. It can be made up wholly of the sense that you, personally, have achieved.

In a boy, too, football expresses and satisfies the warlike instincts, the spirit of defense of hearth and home. He visualizes the rival team as the personification of an ancient enemy. He is conscious of fighting for a bright and a lofty ideal: the defense of Alma Mater and the furtherance of her glory.

The nobler idea of co-operation and protection glows quite as strongly within him, if he is a fine boy, as the pugnacious, competitive instinct. He is willing to go through fire and brimstone, for cherished comrades not only, but even for fellows whom, off the field or out of the playing season, he would be inclined to shun. The football player participates in the high experience of generous physical sacrifice. There is no taint of personal gain. There is always the abundant and natural satisfaction that comes to the normal man or boy of ambition in the accomplishment of things worth while.

There may be men of honorable life and rational thought to whom my portrait of the football player might seem overdrawn, idealized too highly; but is it necessary for a man to limit himself to God, country and fireside in a belief that there are no other ideals worthy, in however less degree, of his love and toil? Surely affection for college or school, or hamlet or city, may be included among the things that are worthy to quicken dreams to deeds;

and football typifies, better than any other game, the successes and setbacks of ideal, manly life, preparing its initiates for both.

So much for the ideal aspects of that which President-Emeritus Tucker of Dartmouth so profoundly characterized as the one great academic game.

The coach must harden himself against occasional moments of disenchantment caused by the discovery that the incentive behind a few of the men who are playing football is quite insufficient to carry them to the real heights of achievement. Perhaps the greatest misfortune to all games is the man who finds himself representing a school or a college in athletics on a firm, well-defined and absolute business basis. On a plane of calamity only a little higher is the player preoccupied with wondering how much extra money he is going to have to spend, or thinking about the job that awaits him if, until he is graduated, he can continue to be a success as a star player. The player in question would be far better fitted for that job, or for a better one, if his mind had not been dwarfed by some such subtle or outright promise of employment, in the gift of another, given without regard to his ability to make good except as an athlete.

I would not wish to go on record as holding that an athlete should lose a legitimate job at college or during vacations because he is an athlete. We are all human — college faculties, alumni and undergraduates are human. I believe in the desire to excel. It stimulates manhood, ambition and civilization. I believe in the enthusiasm of graduates who seek to encourage all worthy youths to enroll themselves at the institution which the older men love and cherish. But for the sake of the young man himself, and his future conscience, I am most strongly opposed to the athlete's receiving make-believe jobs, or presents in the form of money or clothes, donated because he is an athlete.

The unfortunate young man so mistakenly professionalized can never experience the thrill of winning or losing for a high

ideal; and in the days to come can never enjoy the deep satisfactions of him who gave freely of all he had in a good cause,
with never a thought of paltry personal gain. His school or college reunions will lack that elixir which sends his more fortunate
classmate out invigorated and rejuvenated by one more fleeting
hour of contact with his Alma Mater. He will be one of the poor-
est financial contributors to his college; for he will always feel
that he gave more to his college than his college gave to him: a
lamentable mental conclusion.

New coaches, however, must understand at once that there
are certain impedimenta which they have to carry, possibly of
the type already described, almost certainly of another type, one
not wholly lacking in the more humorous aspects which frail hu-
manity presents. I have reference now to the bevy of photograph
football players. Football managers, or at least the photographers,
find it necessary to take a picture of the entire squad before that
squad has been so far reduced as to militate against an extended
sale of the picture. The boys who love to sit in the pictures are
usually present in rather considerable numbers. After the group
picture has been taken, the coach must expect a falling off in
attendance at practice.

He must not permit himself to become too much discouraged.
The absent members have already gone as far with football as they
dare for the small reward of getting into the squad picture. That
reward includes an improved social status at home, and a reputation in the town community, never to be forgotten, of having, in
their youthful days, played on the school or college football team.
It also gives them a distinct advantage over stay-at-home swains
in the competition for the favors of the village belle.

The coach should not regret the instruction he has imparted
to the photograph football players, for at least they have shown
what is, for them, a remarkable depth of feeling, and a certain
degree of admiration for the real football men. Quite possibly

these same photograph players, or some of them, could they be inveigled far enough into the season, might find that they were braver than they knew. For, after all, the amount of courage requisite to play football is not extraordinary. Little by little the novice player learns the habit of taking a chance. Seldom, if ever, come moments to the enthusiastic football player when he may be said to have a desperate chance with time to argue pro and con. The photograph player may be braver than he thinks he is. He may develop, and often has, with much greater courage and love for the game than he ever dared to dream.

The chronic "crab" represents another difficult type which any coach, in sheer self-defense, must learn how to handle. If possible, he should by clever management so arrange that when the "crabbing" begins the other players laugh heartily, much to the surprise and even to the delight of the "crab," whose transition from crabbedness to the state of becoming a genuine wit may date, who knows, from that very moment.

Another effective method is to let the "crab" discover suddenly that he is a great chum of the coach, assistant coach, trainer or whoever can bear him. This relationship usually will cause him to choke whenever he finds himself inclined to indulge in crabbedness. Either he must give up his new chums, which he will never do, being at heart an enthusiast, or cease his fault-finding, and so become a help, rather than a nuisance.

I once had on my team such a chronic gloom that I was forced to associate with him myself, laugh at his outbursts and treat him as a wit. But I very nearly lost my equilibrium one fine sunshiny morning. He entered my rooms with the profanely expressed complaint that he had gone to the trouble of purchasing an exceedingly "classy" raincoat before undertaking his two-thousand-mile journey to play on a football team; and that he'd bet anything the damned weather would continue, thus denying him the slightest opportunity to wear the garment in question.

After I had laughed, and after he had growled and stared, we went down to the field, to begin the last week of the season. He reached the conclusion that at least it was good football weather. And he was the man whose work won the championship game.

Another set of problems is presented by the boy who got into football while attending preparatory school because, being large and strong for his years, he was shamed into playing. Pride and the urging of friends at home carry him. on into college football, but with no marked degree of enthusiasm on his part. His reputation was made on a team where he was bigger than the gang around him. Sometimes he values that reputation so highly that he is afraid to chance it. Often he is a fellow of more than sufficient means and inclined to be lazy. He feels that everything except football will tend to make his college life one grand, sweet song. He loves the old game well enough, but he loves the game as played by others, or as played by himself without physical discomfort.

Therefore he wanders in the lanes of discontent, searching for the incentive to keep him going; or, better still, for the bright and happy avenue of escape. Once he proves his ability to play football, forsooth, the bright and happy avenue of escape is forever blocked by the coach. The coach, in exchange, finds himself, in all fairness, bound to provide the man with incentives, if he can. This is indeed a trying task, though not without its interest. It is, in the first place, absolutely necessary for the coach, like a friendly maggot, to get under the small-school hero's skin. Companionship, cajolery, frequent appeals to pride, even when pride is almost entirely lacking, and sometimes moments of blazing anger must be employed by the guardian coach. Create in the man everlasting respect, and, if possible, admiration, for yourself. Such a man will do more for the individual, oftentimes, than for banquets or for headlines in the newspapers.

The blasé senior, who has had more than his share of the sweets of football accomplishment and applause during a long school or college career, is another fellow who exists for the exasperation of coaches. This man is still able to get up a thrill for a big game, but he has lost his interest in practice, and it often requires demotion to the second eleven to revive it.

There is altogether too great a tendency on the part of the people who claim to be "in the know," and who seldom are, to use rather indiscriminately and often the term "quitter," as applied to football players and to athletes in general. To a man of red blood, this is a terrible epithet; a hopeless brand, which tends to ruin his confidence in himself, and may have very far-reaching and unfortunate results. After eighteen years of active coaching, I confess that I do not know what a quitter is: where to draw the line between the fighter and the quitter I am unable to discover.

Once in a very great while, and out of a thousand football players, a coach will run upon a man whose courage is at all times patently reduced to a rapid retreat. In other words, he is so hopelessly without courage that the puzzling question is how he ever got into football at all. This man, however, is the rarest of exceptions.

On the other hand, out of a thousand players and would-be players I have seldom seen a man who would not do the most extraordinary deeds, if sufficient mental impetus were present. In the same breath I may say that in all these years I believe the men could be counted on the fingers of two hands who have not, or would not, "quit," within the meaning of that unfortunate word, whenever the mental burden became too great. It is not natural for men, except in case of dire necessity, or extreme state of mental elevation, to carry a great burden indefinitely.

Courage is never physical, but always mental; and this is a glorious thought, for it means that the physical giant cannot, by reason of his stature, produce one iota of courage superior to that produced by the most insignificant pigmy. It is one of the lessons of antiquity most profound, most human and most consoling, that the hero who pursues his enemy around the walls of Troy-town is by him pursued, another day. The ancients explained by the intervention of their deities the flaws and fluctuations of the human spirit, hour by hour. We, who are presumably wiser than they, are no less compelled to the conviction, that courage or the lack of it depends not upon girth or length of limb, not upon giant thews or hardness of muscular development. Even Achilles was not brave every day. The giant of yesterday may be the pigmy of the morrow, not because of physical degeneracy, but because of mental change, due to any one of many causes.

Breaking training, whether during season or at the end of it, is a mental change before it becomes a physical act. With imaginative youngsters, the harm done mentally is apt to outweigh considerably the physical effect of violating or terminating the course of training. To break training may indeed be a dark and desperate deed, inwardly, although it only takes the form of eating candy, dancing, sitting in the park or smoking. There are some things worse than others, but whoever breaks training ought at least to realize that even at the end of the season he is delivering a shock to his system by so doing. The system is usually kind enough to stand the shock, or to appear to do so, at the time, but sometimes grim reminders will crop out in the dim, undiscovered future. It is certain, at any rate, that breaking training does not help a foot-ball player to start training another year.

The man who flagrantly and willfully breaks training during season must be dismissed from the squad, whatever his potential ability as a football player. There are occasions when a coach or a trainer can better afford not to be too severe, but with due regard at all times both to discipline and to the welfare of the individual; and with a very special regard to the spirit and disposition of the man who has violated some minor provision of the code. While the rules of strict training may often seem to be unnecessarily severe and restrictive, it is impossible to argue against the spirit of them, which is that men must be willing to make every reasonable sacrifice for a worthy cause. It is in this spirit, and not otherwise, that they command respect and merit enforcement.

It is usually after the coach has the probable makeup of his team fairly well outlined in his own mind that he begins to place himself on a social basis with certain players other than the captain of the team. He will begin to neglect less frequently or even to create opportunities for a chance meeting, or a walk with this player or that. What the coach will then proceed to say to the player depends on what he ought to say to him. As a general rule, you want him, for reasons which you understand better than anyone else, to know at this particular time that you are a human being, and that you have a real interest in him, great as may be his surprise to learn it. Or, you may have some special thing you want to find out, and which is easier to find out if you can put yourself on a friendly social basis with the player, at least for the time being. In another case, it may be that you feel it your duty to give the player a little gossip, disparaging as to himself, which you have received from opposing forces, or believe that you did. This to arouse his ire, or a bit of extra fight, a very difficult thing to arouse, it may be, in this particular man.

Then you have the player whom you discover to be more worldly than most of your football men; who needs to be told that Smith or Jones or Brown, or all three of them, the heads of great business organizations or men who wield vast prestige, are going to be at the game for the special purpose of seeing your young companion "go through big." Or you may impress upon him that many of your friends from home will attend the game, chiefly for the purpose of seeing him in action. As a rule, these things are all true in the particular cases in point. Now and then, however, in order to draw out the best there is in a man, it is necessary to use a certain amount of imagination. While a coach should avoid mixing in fraternity rivalries, and should show himself to be a person of discretion at all times, it is well for him to possess accurate sources of information as to school or college politics, for his better guidance in keeping a firm hold on the players. He should have sufficient influence, at least, if worthy of the name of a good coach, to disparage any politics, while the season is still on, looking toward the election of a captain for next year; or any other politics, in fact. Always I have found that this can be done.

The direct and indirect influence and effect of newspaper publicity, and of the college prints, is deserving of study by thoughtful coaches, who must occasionally intervene to counteract the results of over-praise or of blame not sufficiently deserved. The coach may also have reason to believe that some of his rivals are taking advantage of the power of the press to render certain of their own players more formidable in reputation than in reality, and others less so. Publicity is an aid made use of inadvertently or otherwise by nearly every coach, and the newspapers have a particularly profound influence over the fortunes of coaches who operate near the large centers of population. Scarcely a morning or an evening edition appears without a column telling of the electrifying deeds of some great back, or end, or tackle, now playing on the varsity; whose even more remarkable deeds are being kept under cover until the final game of the season. In spite of all that can be done by their coach to counteract this influence, the players who must eventually encounter this terrible man-eater are inevitably influenced by all this extraordinary publicity. The players read the sporting pages with bulging eyes, and it becomes necessary for the coach to fight fire with fire by disparaging much-touted rivals, and to insist that a hard tackle will bring any of them down to their proper dust.

The "featuring" of certain players is considerably more exaggerated and sensational in football than in sports which contain less of glamour. The custom of holding much of the practice behind closed gates deepens the mystery surrounding football, which grows deeper and darker still, as a rule, when the coaches begin to claim the right of censorship, and even of revision, over the reports of the practice to be sent broadcast. Writers with space to fill are naturally driven to the exercise of their own imaginations if denied free access to sources of reliable information. In this case, however, they are compelled to accept as reliable the information that reaches them, the effect of which on the reader has been carefully calculated, in many instances. I can recall the case of at least one remarkable football specialist, who was kept at a brilliant gait throughout his undergraduate career in football by a studied campaign of propaganda; a subtle head coach continuing to boost him, and to expatiate upon his remarkable qualities, until he managed to hold him almost without suspicion for four years. Secret practice can be just as secret as the coaches care to make it. And in this connection it may be said, for the benefit of young coaches, that a big varsity team is usually ready for its championship games, as regards condition and general offense, two or three weeks before it plays them. Do not scrimmage your team every day, young coach, because the papers say that all the big teams are doing it. Disregard the startling information that any one of these teams has suffered crushing defeat at the hands of its own freshmen eleven, behind the barred gates. Rather brush up on your fundamentals and assignments, going through the same plays day after day. Let fast, snappy signal practice, grass drills and rope drills, or substitutes for them, and the exercise of your own personality, take the place of slavish imitation of what the great varsity elevens are supposed to be doing.

CHAPTER XXXVIII: THE MYSTIC NEXUS

Seldom later than a week before the most important game of the season I have been accustomed to gather the players together for a quiet evening, intending it to be spent in discharging calmly and dispassionately but with all sincerity the pent-up emotions of these hearts young and brave. A mysterious nexus known as college spirit goes round the room that night. Boys whose vehicle of expression is halting and awkward as their spirit is fiery and sincere find somehow the means to make themselves understood by their fellows, until the old, dim banners hung on the gymnasium walls are vague in the fine mist of very precious and sacred tears.

Let it not be understood that on these occasions I excite, permit or share a mere emotional debauch. Unless all the great things are tawdry and false, this get-together evening contains nothing irrational, nothing that may not be regarded reverently. The justification is this. You have in your squad players whose boyish hearts are swelling almost to the bursting point; and others, perchance, who have never attuned themselves to the celestial music. At the height of the football season you will find one thing or another, but mawkishness or insincerity seldom. This is the occasion, in my experience, when comrades, chums and good pals find themselves brothers; when the cold, distant, standoffish chap is discovered almost visibly to have a heart of gold; when the schemer's hard fibers are touched, and his premature, false cynicism falls from him like a ragged garment, discarded perhaps forever.

"College Spirit"
Harris & Ewing

There is a wonderful power in strong, modulated, earnest voices, as young men tell one another what college spirit really means to them; of the joys and thrills of football; of sacrifices willingly made; of fealty joyfully pledged; of a win and a bonfire and a ball for the trophy case as their all-sufficing longed-for reward for everything that they have endured.

These meetings are intended, frankly, to develop team and college spirit, for the sake of winning; but there is also and always the deep satisfaction that you have taken one of the last real opportunities to put into the hearts of these children something like the enduring fragrance of flowers; an imperishable memory, persisting in the sordid and self-seeking atmosphere of the huckster world beyond the quadrangle. I have seen them turn to their rest with faces hushed and hallowed; and I believe, as they, that the august spirit of their Alma Mater stood guard beside them through the watches of the night.

The End

"MAJOR FRANK W. CAVANAUGH"

Francis William Cavanaugh was born in Worcester, Massachusetts on April 28th, 1876 to Patrick Cavanaugh and Ann O'Brien
Cavanaugh, both Irish immigrants. A star football player in high
school, Cavanaugh later attended Dartmouth where he continued
to excel at the game. In 1898 Cavanaugh left Dartmouth to accept
a job at the University of Cincinnati, the first in a series of increasingly successful coaching positions he would hold until his
untimely death in 1933.

Major Frank W. Cavanaugh

After a year in Cincinnati, Cavanaugh headed west for a three-
year stint with the Denver Athletic Club. Returning to Worcester,

he coached at Worcester High School, Worcester Academy and at Holy Cross. Cavanaugh had left Dartmouth without graduating, but after returning to Worcester he found time to study law at Boston College. In spite of obtaining a law degree in 1903, Cavanaugh's commitment to practicing his profession apparently remained on the football field.

A turning point in his career came in 1911 when Cavanaugh was hired to lead the Dartmouth football team. Cavanaugh served as head coach at Dartmouth until 1916. During this period he built a solid reputation, leading his team to an impressive 42-9-3 record over six seasons. In spite of his accomplishments at Dartmouth, Cavanaugh was forced to resign with a year left on his contract, reportedly owing to differences with the administration regarding the future direction of football at the college.

The following year would reveal as much about Cavanaugh's character as any game on any field in any season. When the United States of America entered the ongoing war in Europe, Francis William Cavanaugh, a husband, father, and then forty-one years of age, joined the army and marched off to France. "Cav" Cavanaugh quickly rose through the ranks. On October 23rd, 1918, while in command of the 2nd Battalion of the 102nd Field Artillery, Captain Cavanaugh was grievously wounded when an enemy artillery shell struck his command dugout. Cavanaugh would leave the war with the rank of Major.

After the war Cavanaugh spent a year coaching in Omaha, Nebraska before returning to Massachusetts, where he was named head coach at Boston College. Beginning in 1919, the year which saw publication of *Inside Football*, Cavanaugh led the Boston College Eagles to an eight season record of 48-14-5. After his tenure at Boston College, Cavanaugh would go on to coach the Fordham Rams with a record of 34-14-4 during the years 1927-1932. Over a twenty-four-year career in college football, Cavanaugh's record was 145-48-17, a career average of .731 percent.

Toward the end of 1932, failing health and loss of vision due to shrapnel wounds suffered during the war would force Cavanaugh to retire from the field. He died at home, surrounded by his family, on August 29th, 1933, and was buried at St. John's Cemetery in Worcester.

Cavanaugh's life and career were depicted in the 1943 Hollywood film, "The Iron Major," starring the popular 20th century Irish-American actor Pat O'Brien in the title role.

Coach Frank W. Cavanaugh was inducted into the College Football Hall of Fame in 1954.

SOURCES

TEXT

The text of this edition is reproduced from the first edition of *Inside Football* by Frank W. Cavanaugh, published in Boston by Small Maynard and Company in 1919.

The biographical sketch appended to the end of this edition is by Ether Editors. Details about Francis William Cavanaugh's life and career are from his obituary as it appeared in the *New York Times* on August 30th, 1933 (p. 19). His military exploits are documented in the regimental history *An American Battery in France* by Corporal Ernest E. La Branche, published by the Belisle Printing and Publishing Company of Worcester, Massachusetts in 1923. Cavanaugh's statistical record is documented in the National Football Foundation's College Football Hall of Fame.

ILLUSTRATIONS

The illustrations appearing in this edition of Frank W. Cavanaugh's *Inside Football* are from the collections of the Library of Congress in Washington, D.C. The illustrations are from the early 1900s to the 1920s. Photographic illustrations are of several different college football teams, including Carlisle, Dartmouth, Georgetown, and Harvard. Illustrations from "Puck" originally appeared in color and have been rendered here in black and white. Each illustration has been modified (cropping, resizing, retouching). Most have been titled or retitled by Ether Editors to suit the present edition.

Readers may access the original illustrations via the Library of Congress Prints and Photographs Division. Seach the Library of Congress website [https://www.loc.gov] using the Library of Congress Control Number [LCCN] associated with each illustration.

––––––––––

"Dartmouth Football Team" | [Cover Illustration] | [LCCN-2013646099] | Credit: H.H.H. Langill

"Tackling Dummy" | [Chapter III: Page 15] | [LCCN-2014690938] | Credit: Bain News Service

"Line Up for a Punt-Out!" | [Chapter IV: Page 19] | [LCCN-2016888192] | Credit: Harris & Ewing

"Grass Drill" | [Chapter V: Page 25] | [LCCN-2016891724] | Credit: Harris & Ewing

"Exercise" | [Chapter VI: Page 41] | [LCCN-2014689714] | Credit: Bain News Service

"Line Defense" | [Chapter IX: Page 52] | [LCCN-2013645853] | Credit: National Photo Company

"Carlisle vs. Dartmouth" | [Chapter XV: Page 91] | [LCCN-2014694811] | Credit: Bain News Service

"If an End Had Four Eyes..." | [Chapter XVII: Page 101] | [LCCN-2013645852] | Credit: National Photo Company

"Runner on the Field" | [Chapter XX: Page 119] | [LCCN-2016893873] | Credit: Harris & Ewing

"Not So Bad" | [Chapter XXI: Page 125] | [LCCN-2012647392] | Credit: Frank A. Nankivell in "Puck"

"Sideline Play" | [Chapter XXII: Page 132] | [LCCN-2016892854] | Credit: Harris & Ewing

"Gee, But You Look Funny!" (A Political Cartoon) | [Chapter XXV: Page 156] | [LCCN-2011649399] | Credit: Will Crawford in "Puck"

"One Side, Please!" | [Chapter XXVI: Page 164] | [LCCN-2016682328] | Credit: Herbert Johnson for Associated Newspapers

"A Good Kicker" | [Chapter XXVII: Page 175] | [LCCN-2002714416] | Credit: Unidentified Contributor

"Future Players" | [Chapter XXXI: Page 206] | [LCCN-2016863113] | Credit: Harris & Ewing

"Guardians of the Ball" | [Chapter XXXV: Page 238] | [LCCN-2016892852] | Credit: Harris & Ewing

"Dartmouth Football Team" | [Chapter XXXVI: Page 244] | [LCCN-2013646099] | Credit: H.H.H. Langill

"College Spirit" | [Chapter XXXVIII: Page 264] | [LCCN-2016893910] | Credit: Harris & Ewing

"Major Frank W. Cavanaugh" | [Page 267] | Credit: Unidentified Contributor [From the First Edition of *Inside Football*]

COLOPHON

ETHER EDITIONS
Futurum est in aethere

PUBLISHED BY ETHER EDITIONS

Caricatures by Gene Markey

In Praise of Folly by Desiderius Erasmus

Inside Football by Frank W. Cavanaugh

King of the Black Isles by J. U. Nicolson

The Smart Set Conversations
by H. L. Mencken and George Jean Nathan

www.ingramcontent.com/pod-product-compliance
Lightning Source LLC
Chambersburg PA
CBHW070910120626
46546CB00001B/207